SHAKESPEARE'S JEST BOOK

Shakespeare's Jest Book

An Edition of

A Hundred Mery Talys (1526)

Edited in 1866

By

Hermann Oesterley

A Facsimile Reproduction

With an Introduction

By

Leonard R. N. Ashley

> Buy, reade, and judge,
> The price do not grudge;
> It will do thee more pleasure,
> Than twice so much treasure. —
> *Merrie and Conceited Jests
> of George Peele*, 1607.

GAINESVILLE, FLORIDA

SCHOLARS' FACSIMILES & REPRINTS

1970

Scholars' Facsimiles & Reprints
1605 N. W. 14th Avenue
Gainesville, Florida 32601, U.S.A.
Harry R. Warfel, General Editor

For
HUNDLEY THOMPSON, JR.

Reproduced from a Copy in
and with the permission of
The British Museum

L. C. Catalog Card Number: 70-133328

ISBN 8201-1083-3

Manufactured in the U.S.A.

INTRODUCTION

The jester was always one of the most significant persons at court in medieval and Renaissance Europe, and humor was one of the best keys to the understanding of the society. The *marotte* or bauble of the jester was often a symbol of power. Winnow all the folly of a shrewd man in motley, as Sir W. S. Gilbert suggested, and there will be "a grain or two of truth among the chaff." The jester's wit gives cheer to the lowly and restores a sense of proportion to the powerful. When comedy strives, as in Jonson's satires, to "show an image of the times/And sport with human follies, not with crimes" it serves an essential social purpose.

Shakespeare, who studied the function of the fool both in jestbooks of foreign origin (such as *Fables of Alfonce and Poge*, 1484, and versions of the Til Eulenspiegel or *Howleglas* stories) and of English composition (such as Thomas Berthelet's *Tales and Quicke Answers*, c. 1535), was also able to draw on the living tradition of his clowns Will Kempe and Robert Armin, adapting the jester to such diverse purposes as the enlivening of his comedies and the deepening of the tragedy in *King Lear*. At command were both the lively theatrical tradition of the clown and a library of jestbooks from the pens of James Sandforde, Thomas Twyne, Phiston, Richard Tarleton, Sir Richard Barclay, John Singer, Giles Corrozet, Thomas Dekker, George Wilkins, Richard

Johnson, and many an anonymous author or collector of "clinches, bulls, quirkes, yerkes, quips and jerkes" assembled, as Thomas Deloney said in his *Mirror of Mirth and Pleasant Conceits* (1583), for "the recreation and delight of many, and to the hurt and hinderance of none," whether old chestnuts or new jokes, designed to prepare the reader to scintillate in public or to relax in private.

A Hundred Mery Talys (1526) was one of these treasuries of the humor of the common man that Shakespeare certainly knew and employed. Hermann Oesterley recounts something of the history of the book; it may be added that a third copy has been found and is now in the Folger Shakespeare Library. The three extant copies seem to belong to two different editions. Certainly this collection, though only one of many (as the lists of Ernest Schulz in *Palestra,* CXVII; F. P. Wilson in *Huntington Library Quarterly,* II; and P. M. Zall in *Shakespearean Research Opportunities,* VI, demonstrate), was important enough to have John Rastell's rights assigned in 1557/8 to John Walley and in 1582 to Samson Awdley and John Charlwood. If these men issued new editions, they apparently are lost.

In *A Hundred Mery Talys,* as well as other collections of quips, answers (riddles), and anecdotes, there is a link between the great dramatist's art, in tragedy and festive comedy both, and the folk wisdom and fun handed down from generation to generation. Among the happy hodgepodge of *A Hundred Mery Talys,* derived from a great many old and foreign sources, there is plenty of domestic wit and wisdom from the court and the alehouse, native funny stories that were the common property of the period. Probably the principal milestone in the development of the jestbook in England from Caxton's time to Shakespeare's, *A Hundred Mery Talys* presents this humorous trove in a simple, charming, colloquial style. Here may be heard the authentic voice of the common people, the penny public of Shakespeare's theatre, in the crude, sometimes clever little stories that have the direct and naïve appeal of woodcuts, fresh and striking. There are many other jestbooks, but probably there is none which can equal this one in importance—and very few are anywhere near as entertaining.

LEONARD R. N. ASHLEY

Brooklyn College of
The City University of New York
March, 1970

Shakespeare's Jest Book.

A HUNDRED MERY TALYS,

FROM THE ONLY PERFECT

COPY KNOWN.

EDITED,

WITH INTRODUCTION AND NOTES,

BY

DR. HERMAN OESTERLEY.

LONDON:
JOHN RUSSELL SMITH,
SOHO SQUARE.
1866.

INTRODUCTION.

HE editor of the following pages, while engaged in the compofition of a new catalogue of the profe works of fiction preferved in the Royal Library of the Univerfity in Göttingen, met with a perfect copy of the "C. Merry Tales," printed by John Raftell in 1526. He poftponed, however, all refearches regarding it until the time when the advancement of his work fhould require. In the mean time this copy came under the notice of Dr. Carl Goedeke, the eminent judge of early literature, who at once recognized it as the book alluded to by Shakefpeare in "Much Ado About Nothing." This caufed my learned colleague, Prof. F. W. Unger, to give a bibliographical account of the difcovery in the "Serapeum" (No. 9, May 15th, 1864, p. 142). About this time, Mr. Hazlitt's reprint from the fragmentary but until this time only known copy reached us,[1] and notice was given of it in the " Göttinger gelehrte Anzeigen " (23 St. June 8th, 1864, p. 917) by Prof. Unger, thus again drawing the attention of literary men to the perfect copy preserved in our library.

The original of Mr. Hazlitt's edition was discovered by the Rev. J. J. Conybeare in 1815,[2] and reprinted the fame year in S. W. Singer's " Jeft Book."[3] It was printed without date,

[1] " Shakefpeare Jeft Books; reprints of the early and very rare Jeft Books fuppofed to have been ufed by Shakefpeare. I. A Hundred Mery Talys. II. Mery Tales and Quicke Anfweres. Edited, with Introduction and Notes, by W. Carew Hazlitt. London, Willis and Sotheran, 1864, 8º."

[2] Collier, " Shakefpeare," Lond. 1842, vol. ii. p. 208, note 8, gives erroneously the year 1835 as the date of the difcovery and reprint.

[3] " Shakefpeare Jeft Book. Part I. Tales and quicke Anfweres very mery and pleafant to rede, with a Preface and a Gloffary. Part II. A C mery Talys, with a Preface and a Gloffary. Part III. Supplement to the Tales and quicke Anfweres, being Mery Tales, wittie Queftions and quicke Anfweres, very pleafant to be readde." Chifwick, 1814-16, 8vo. Three parts in 1 vol., 250 copies printed, with an " Addrefs to the Reader," by the editor, S. W. Singer, Efq. Of this edition hardly a fingle copy has ever come to Germany. See " Biographical Memoir of Edmond Malone" [by James Bofwell], Lond. 1814, privately

INTRODUCTION.

but with the mark of John Raſtell[4] on the reverſe of the laſt leaf, twenty-four leaves in folio, black letter.[5] Many leaves of this copy, from having been uſed as paſteboard to another book, were mutilated, and though ſeveral copies had been employed in faſhioning the paſteboard, and ſo a comparatively large fragment was ſaved, yet many deficiencies remained. Beſides a quantity of ſmaller gaps throughout the whole book, in twenty-ſix[6] of the tales ſeveral lines are wanting, and ſix[7] are too much damaged to decypher.

The original of the preſent edition is perfect. It was printed by John Raſtell in 1526, black letter, twenty-eight leaves in folio, though only

---

printed; "Retroſpective Review," N. S. No. 8, Aug. 1854, vol. ii. p. 313; "London Magazine," edited by Taylor and Heſſey, 1823-24.

[4] See, about this early Engliſh printer, James Ames, "Typographical Antiquities," augmented by W. Herbert, Lond. 1785-90, 4to. vol. i. p. 326.

[5] Lowndes, "The Bibliographer's Manual," part v. p. 1200, mentions the 18mo. ſize. For further particulars, ſee Mr. Hazlitt's edition, Introduction, p. iii. ſeq.

[6] Viz. Nos. 3, 4, 22, 24, 42, 46, 47, 49, 52, 53, 55, 59, 60, 63, 64, 67, 69, 74, 77, 81, 83, 87, 91, 94, 96, 100.

[7] Viz. Nos. 26, 35, 72, 78, 84, 95, correſponding to Nos. 28, 36, 74, 80, 86, 99 of this edition.

vi   *INTRODUCTION.*

twenty-ſix numbered, including title and table. It contains E iii by ſignatures, the firſt ſheet in fours, the remainder in ſixes. The front of the firſt leaf is without ſignature and bears in xylographic frame-work the title, " A .C. mery talys;" on the back of the leaf begins " the kalender" or the table of the tales, which is continued on the ſecond leaf A ii. Then follow folios 1 to 26,[1] containing the text of the tales. The ſtories are without headings or numbers, generally with a moral attached and a break in type between each. The firſt letter of each ſtory is printed ſeparately, moſt of them in a ſquare for illumination. The text finiſhes upon the firſt page of the laſt leaf with the word " Finis;" on the reverſe follows the Colophon and the mark of *John Raſtell* in large frame-work, and under it: *Cum preuilegio Regali.*

According to an entry in the Library's Manual of the year 1768[2] this copy has been purchaſed at an auction of books in Lüneburg, December,

---

[1] Fol. 2 and 26 bear erroneouſly the numbers 26 and reſp. 21.

[2] "Manuale," 1768. Angekommen d. 13 Jan. p. 6. Aus der Auction eines Vorraths von Büchern, welche am 7 Dec. 1767 u. f. zu Lüneburg in Peterſens Hauſe an den Meiſtbietenden ſollen verkauft werden, p. 9, 145, No. 2. " A C mery talys." Lond. 1526, (Acc. f. 5368.)

INTRODUCTION. vii

1767; but I have been unfuccefsful in tracing its hiftory further back.

The differences between this impreffion and the one edited by Singer and reprinted by Mr. Hazlitt are very confiderable. Our edition has four tales which are not contained in the undated copy, viz. Nos. 2, 7, 91 and 98; for which at the end of the latter three new ftories are added, Nos. 97, 99 and 100. No. 98 is wanting in the table as well as in the text of Mr. Hazlitt's edition, and as he does not give any reafon of this ftriking deficiency, nor even mention it, I am unable to decide whether it arifes from a negligence of the original compiler, from a lacuna in the only preferved copy, or from an error of the later editors; the lefs, as Mr. Singer's reprint is faid to be nearly an accurate facfimile of the original, and Mr. Hazlitt profeffes to have rigidly adhered even to the old orthography.

Again, in Mr. Hazlitt's edition the morals of Nos. 34, 79 and 96 are wanting, correfponding to Nos. 35, 81 and 100 of the prefent edition; and further is No. 43 of our original No. 33 of the undated copy.

For fmaller variations I may firft refer to the kalender or table. In the beginning the headings are entirely different, but afterwards, with the exception perhaps of Nos. 44 and 66 (Nos. 42

and 64 in Haz.), only very trifling alterations of single words occur.

The variations of the two editions in single phrases and expressions of the text are numerous, and they are, after careful collation, noted under the text, excepting those, however, which have arisen from the interpolations of the later editors.

Finally, the difference of orthography and punctuation might be mentioned, but for the capriciousness of the orthography in both editions, and for the thorough modernizing of the punctuation in Mr. Hazlitt's edition, the only one at my command.

The question, which of the two copies recovered up to the present moment is the original and older edition (and there is very little hope of ever discovering a third copy), will be very difficult to prove to an absolute certainty. By the want of any authentic indication, the inquiry is thrown back on a mere circumstantial proof; but I think the reasons to be given hereafter will be strong enough to produce a firm conviction of the priority of our original.

The first argument in favour of the edition of 1526 is founded on the selection and disposition of the tales. When a reprint of a collection of a hundred tales like the one in question is being prepared, and the removing of four stories seems desirable, it is unlikely enough, that the three or four last pieces should be cast off; but it is much more unlikely that the number required to complete a hundred should be inserted in entirely chance places. This, however, would have been the case in the Nos. 2, 7, 91 and 98 of our edition, if it had been a revision of the undated copy. On the other hand, it is quite natural simply to throw out the tales considered as unserviceable (which, as before mentioned, would hardly be placed together, but be scattered throughout the work) and to subjoin the additions at the end. This has been the case, if the undated edition is the result of a revision: Nos. 2, 7, 91 and 98 of the original edition have been suppressed, and in their stead Nos. 97 to 100 of the later impression are added. I must say, that this mode of revision, in a work where the disposition of the matter is entirely arbitrary, seems to me more natural than even putting the new stories in the place of the old ones. The substance of the tales in discussion can be of no moment for the question, for indeed, the one is about as insipid as the other, and moreover, the taste of our ancestors in regard to jests and popular tales was so very different from ours, that it is next to impossible at present to decide which of them

INTRODUCTION.

might be confidered more palatable to the public at that time.

The tranfpofition of a fingle tale to another place[1] can, of courfe, be no conclufive argument either for one view or for the other, whereas the want of the morals in the undated copy is of confequence, if it really be found in the original and not be produced by a defect, which is not quite evident in Mr. Hazlitt's reprint. As our copy contains twenty-eight leaves and the undated one only twenty-four, therefore the arrangement of the type in each muft have been quite different; the abfence of thefe morals might have arifen from a defire of faving fpace, and thus furnifh a new evidence for the priority of the dated edition.

The variations in the table favour my opinion in an equal manner. Wherever any effential differences occur in the headings, they are equal to as many emendations in the undated copy,[2] and thefe improvements evidently bear witnefs to the later appearance of the revifed edition; the more, as there is no trace of a third edition earlier than both, of which the undated copy might poffibly be a revifed impreffion, ours being only a later and unrevifed reprint.

[1] No. 43 to No. 33 of the undated edition.
[2] See the headings of Nos. 1 to 6, 44 and 66.

INTRODUCTION. xi

This might, indeed, have been the cafe for the alterations of the text; but under the circumftances it is too improbable to be advanced as an objection, and I may fairly put it out of the queftion. Among the very large quantity of variations in the text, there are, of courfe, many entirely irrelevant in the decifion of the queftion, as they cannot be confidered as improvements. The greater part, neverthelefs, proves that the undated edition is the product of a revifion. In the firft place the mifprints are important. The typographical errors of our edition, about fifty or fixty, have all been corrected in Mr. Hazlitt's original, in which, however, there are about twenty new mifprints. The moft remarkable of thefe is p. 35, l. 13 of Mr. Hazlitt's reprint, where evidently from the repetition of the words "tyed faft by the leggys" in three confecutive lines (at the top of fol. vi verfo of our original) more than a line of our text has been omitted, the paffage ending with the firft repetition of thofe words being left out. As it would be impoffible to enumerate all the paffages which go to prove my propofition, I mention only fome of the moft ftriking inftances. Fol. 1 verfo, l. 39, the words "his neck," accidentally omitted in ours, are fupplied in Mr. Hazlitt's edition; fol. 2 verfo, l. 10, "for that that"—Hazl. "becaufe;" fol. 10,

l. 38, " by vyolence"—Hazl. " of the houfe;" fol. 11 verfo, l. 16, " thy"—Hazl. " your;" fol. 14, l. 27, " vp through"—Hazl. " throughe it," &c; but efpecially fol. 21, l. 3 and 4, a very corrupt paffage of our text has been corrected in Mr. Hazlitt's edition, p. 102, l. 8; fol. 23, l. 2, the words " fayde in fporte" are omitted, but have been inferted in the undated copy.

On the other hand, I feel obliged to mention that a few of the variations in the undated copy cannot well be confidered as corrections from our text, but rather feem to indicate the reverfe;[1] this, however, is eafily enough accounted for by the fact that alterations are not always improvements: indeed, in one inftance[2] the very corruption of the text proves its being a revifed edition.

The orthography in both editions is too varied and unfettled to be of any moment for our queftion, although the frequent ufe of written numbers in the undated copy inftead of the fimple cypher, and perhaps the employing of the word " pence" for our abbreviation d. feem to ftrengthen my argument. On the whole, all

[1] F. e. fol. 12, l. 34; fol. 12 verfo, l. 27; fol. 16 verfo, l. 23; fol. 20, l. 21, &c.

[2] Fol. 20 verfo, l. 9; fee the notes.

INTRODUCTION.

the orthography proves is that only a few years elapſed between the appearance of the two editions.

Theſe are the arguments I have to preſent; although each taken ſingly may not be conſidered concluſive, the whole will form as unexceptionable a proof of the priority of our edition as can be expected, and this proof is the more cogent, as there is nothing worth mentioning to be offered in favour of the other edition.

The notes added to the preſent edition do not in any way pretend to contain all that might be collated in regard to the ſources and imitations of the " C Mery Talys." It has certainly been my endeavour to make this collection of parallels as entire as poſſible, but, of courſe, it was only the material at my command which I could call into requiſition; and although this material was uncommonly copious, I have no doubt in a complete collection, eſpecially of Engliſh Jeſt Books, much more might have been gathered. However, many of the Merry Tales bear too unmiſtakeably the ſtamp of originality to leave any hope of tracing their origin farther, and a large number we may ſafely ſuppoſe have never been transferred to the collections of a later period. This forms the eſſential diſtinction between the preſent and moſt of the other Engliſh Jeſt Books, ours being the only one (within my knowledge, at leaſt) containing tales upon the origin or diſſemination of which authentic information cannot be obtained.

It only remains for me to expreſs my ſincereſt thanks to my learned friend, Dr. Carl Goedeke, for the highly valuable aſſiſtance he has furniſhed me in the accompliſhment of my work.

CONTENTS.

                                                    Page

I. Of the mylner that fayd he harde neuer but of ii commaundemens and .ii. dowtys   1
II. Of the cytefen that callyd the preſt ſyr Johñ & he callyd him maſter raf   2
III. Of the wyfe that mayd hyr huſbande to go ſyt in the herber in the nyght while her prentys lay with her in her bed   3
IV. Of hym that playd the deuyll and came thorow the waren & mayd theym that ſtale the connys to ronne away   7
V. Of the ſyk man that bequethyd hys thyrd ſon a lytyll ground with the galows   11
VI. Of the gentylman that loſt his ryng in the gentylwomans bed, & a nother gentylman found it after in the ſame bed   13
VII. Of the huſband man that aſked for maſter pyſpot the phyſyſyon   14
VIII. Of the ſcoler that bare his ſhoys to cloutyng .   17
IX. Of hym that ſayd that a womans tong was lightiſt met of degeſtion   18
X. Of the woman that folowyd her fourth huſbandys herce & wept   19

CONTENTS.

		Page
xi.	Of the woman that fayd her wooer came too late	20
xii	Of the mylner with the golden thombe	22
xiii.	Of the horfman of yrelond that prayd Oconer to hang vp the frere	22
xiv.	Of the preſt that fayd nother corpus meus nor corpum meum	25
xv.	Of the .ii. frerys wherof the one louyd not the ele hed nor the other the tayle	26
xvi.	Of the welchman that ſhroue hym for brekyng his faſt on the fryday	27
xvii.	Of the merchaunt of london that put nobles in his mouth in his deth bed	30
xviii.	Of the mylner that ſtale the nuttys & of the taylér that ſtale a ſhepe	31
xix.	Of the .iiii. elementys where they ſhulde ſone be found	37
xx.	Of the woman that powryd the potage in the Juggys male	39
xxi.	Of the weddyd men that cam to heuyn to clayme theyr herytage	41
xxii.	Of the merchaunte that chargyd hys ſonne to fynde one to ſynge for hys ſowle	42
xxiii.	Of the mayd waſhyng clothys and anſwered the frere	44
xxiv.	Of the .iii. wyfe men of gotam	45
xxv.	Of the gray frere that anſweryd his penytent	47
xxvi.	Of the gentylman that bare the ſege borde on his nek	47
xxvii.	Of the marchauntys wyfe that feyd ſhe wolde take a nap at ſermon	51
xxviii.	Of the woman that feyd & ſhe lyffyd a nother yere ſhe wolde haue a kokoldis hat of her owne	52

CONTENTS. xvii

		Page
xxix.	Of the gentylman that wyſhyd his toth in the gentylwomans tayle	53
xxx.	Of the welchman that confeſſyd hym how he had ſlayn a frere	54
xxxi.	Of the welchman that cowde not get but a lytyll male	55
xxxii.	Of the gentyll woman that ſayd to a gentylman ye haue a berde a boue & none benethe	57
xxxiii.	Of the frere that ſayd our lord fed .v. M. peple with .ij. fyſhys	58
xxxiv.	Of the frankelyne that wold haue had the frere gon	59
xxxv.	Of the good man that ſayd to his wyfe he had yll fare	60
xxxvi.	Of the frere that bad hys chylde make a laten	61
xxxvii.	Of the gentylman that aſkyd the frere for his beuer	62
xxxviii.	Of the .iii. men that chaſe the woman	63
xxxix.	Of the gentylman that taught his cooke the medeſyne for the tothake	65
xl.	Of the gentylman that promyſyd the ſcoler of Oxford a ſarcenet typet	67
xli.	Of maſter ſkelton that brought the byſhop of Norwich .ii. feſantys	70
xlii.	Of the yeman of gard that ſayd he wold bete the carter	73
xliii.	Of the pryſt that ſayd our lady was not ſo curyous a woman	75
xliv.	Of the fole that wold go to the deuyll	76
xlv.	Of the plowmannys ſonne that ſayd he ſaw one make a Goſe to kreke ſweetly	77

b

CONTENTS.

		Page
XLVI.	Of the maydys anfwere that was with chylde	78
XLVII.	Of the feruant that rymyd with his mafter .	79
XLVIII.	Of the welchman that delyueryd the letter to the ape	81
XLIX.	Of hym that fold ryght nought	83
L.	Of the frere that told the iii. chylders fortunys	86
LI.	Of the boy that bare the frere hys mafters money	88
LII.	Of Phylyp fpencer the bochers man	89
LIII.	Of the courtear and the carter.	91
LIV.	Of the yonge man that prayd his felow to tech hym his pater nofter.	91
LV.	Of the frere that prechyd in ryme expownyng the aue maria	93
LVI.	Of the curat that prechyd the artycles of the Crede.	96
LVII.	Of the frere that prechyd the .x. comaundementys.	100
LVIII.	Of the wyfe that bad her hufband ete the candell furft .	103
LIX.	Of the man of lawys fonnys anfwer	104
LX.	Of the frere in the pulpit that bad the woman leue her babelyng	104
LXI.	Of the welchman that caft the fkot in to the fee.	106
LXII.	Of the man that had the dome wyfe	107
LXIII.	Of the proctor of arches that had the lytell wyfe	109
LXIV.	Of the .ii. nonnys that were fhryuyn of one preft	110
LXV.	Of the efquyer that fholde haue bene made knyght	112

CONTENTS.

		Page
LXVI.	Of the man that wold haue the pot ſtand there as he wold	114
LXVII.	Of the penytent that ſayd the ſhepe of god haue mercy vpon me.	116
LXVIII.	¶ Of the huſband that ſayd he was Johñ daw	117
LXIX.	¶ Of the ſkoler of oxford that prouyd by ſoupheſtry .ii. chekyns .iii.	118
LXX.	¶ Of the frere that ſtale the podyng . .	120
LXXI.	Of the frankelyns ſon that cam to take orders	122
LXXII.	Of the huſbandman that lodgyd the frere in hys owne bed	124
LXXIII.	Of the preſt that wold ſay .ii. goſpels for a grote.	125
LXXIV.	Of the courtear that dyd caſt the frere ouer the bote.	126
LXXV.	Of the frere that prechyd what mennys ſowlys were.	127
LXXVI.	Of the huſband that cryed ble vnder the bed	128
LXXVII.	Of the ſhomaker that aſkyd the colyer what tydyngys in hell	130
LXXVIII.	Of ſeynt Peter that cryed cauſe bobe . .	131
LXXIX.	Of hym that aduenturyd body & ſowle for hys prynce	132
LXXX.	Of the parſon that ſtall the mylners elys .	133
LXXXI.	Of the welchman that ſaw one .xl. ſhyl. better than god	134
LXXXII.	Of the frere that ſayd dyrige for the hoggys ſowle.	134
LXXXIII.	Of the parſon that ſayd maſſe of requiem for Cryſtys ſowle	136

CONTENTS.

		Page
LXXXIV.	Of the herdman that fayd ryde apace ye fhall haue rayn	138
LXXXV.	Of hym that fayd I fhall haue nere a peny	139
LXXXVI.	Of the hufband that fayd his wyfe and he agreed well	140
LXXXVII.	Of the preeft that fayd comede epifcope	141
LXXXVIII.	Of the woman that ftale the pot	142
LXXXIX.	Of mafter whyttyntons dreme	143
XC.	Of the preft that kyllyd hys horfe callyd modicum	144
XCI.	Of the maltman of Colbroke	145
XCII.	Of the welchman that ftale the englyfhmans cok	150
XCIII.	Of hym that brought a botell to a preft	150
XCIV.	Of the endytement of Jhefu of Nazareth	151
XCV.	Of hym that prechyd agaynft theym that rode on the fonday	152
XCVI.	Of the one brother that founde a purs	153
XCVII.	Of the anfwere of the mafters to the mayd	155
XCVIII.	Of a certayn aldermans dedys of london	155
XCIX.	Of the northern man that was all hart	158
C.	Of the burnyng of old John	158

A HUNDRED MERY TALYS.

1. Of the mylner that fayd he harde neuer but of ii commaūdemens and .ii. dowtys.

CERTAYN Curat in the contrey there was that prechedin the pulpit of the ten commandementys. Seyng that there were ten cōmaūdemētes that euery man ought to kepe/ & he that brake any of thē/ cōmytted greuous fyn/[1] how be it he fayd that fomtyme it was dedly fyn & fomtyme venyall/ But when it was dedly fyn & when venyall/ there were many douts therin. And a mylner a yong mā a mad felow that cam feldom to church/[2] & had ben at very fewe fermons or none in all his lyfe anfwerd hym thā fhortly this wyfe. I meruel mafter parfon that ye fay ther be fo many cōmaūdemētis & fo many doutys. For I neuer hard tell but of ii.

[1] *greuous fyn*] Hazl. fyn.   [2] *church*] Orig. reads chnrch.

cōmandemēts that is to ſay cōmande me to you and cōmaũde me fro you. Nor I neuer herd tell of mo¹ doutis but twayn that ys to ſay dout² the candell and dout the fyre. At which anſwere all the people fell a laughynge.

¶ By this tale a man may well pceyue that they that be brought vp without lernyng³ or good maner ſhall neuer be but rude and beſtely all though they haue good naturall wyttys.

II. *Of the cyteſen that callyd the preſt ſyr Johñ & he called hĩ maſter raf.*
Wanting in Hazlitt's edition.

ON a tyme there was a Joly Citeſyn walkyng in the cōtrey for ſport which met with a folyſh preſt/ & in diryſyõ in comunycaciõ cald hym ſyr Johñ. this preſt vnderſtonding his mockyng calde him maſter rafe/ why quod the cyteſyn doſte thou call me maſter rafe/ mary quod the preſt why callyſt me ſyr Johñ. Then quod the cyteſen I call the ſyr Johñ becawſe euery folyſh preſte moſt comonly is calde ſir John/ Mary quod the preſt & I call the maſter rafe becauſe eueryproud

¹ *mo*] Hazl. more.   ² *dout*] i. e. fear.
³ *vp without lernyng*] Orig. reads vpwith out leryng.

Cocold moſt comenly is callyd maſter Rafe. At the which anſwer all that were by laught a pace becauſe dyuers there ſuppoſyd the ſame cyteſen to be a cokcold in dede.

¶ By thys tale ye may ſe that he that delyteth[4] to deryde & laughe other to ſkorne is ſomtyme hym ſelfe more derydyd.

III. *Of the wyfe that mayd hyr huſbande to go ſyt in the herber in the nyght whyle her prentys lay with her in her bed.*

The ſources as well as the imitations of this ſtory are very numerous. It ſeems to be modelled after Boccaccio, "Il Decamerone," giorn. vii. nov. 7, or perhaps after the "Cent Nouvelles Nouvelles," nouv. 88. But its real origin is a French fabliau, either "La bourgeoiſe d'Orléans," in Legrand d'Auſſy,"Fabliaux ou Contes du XII. et du XIII.ſiècle," Paris, 1779, tom. iii. p. 411 (alſo in Barbazan-Méon, "Fabliaux et Contes," Paris, 1808, p. 161); or "Raymond Vidal," in Raynouard, "Choix des Poéſies originales des Troubadours," Paris, 1816-1819, tom. iii. p. 398. Likewiſe it is contained in "Poggii facetiæ," s. l. & a. fol: "de muliere quæ virum defraudavit," fol. v. verſo; in Mone's "Anzeiger für Kunde des deutſchen Mittelalters," iv. 453; "Der Herr und der Schreiber;" in Von der Hagen, "Geſammtabenteuer," No. 27; "Frauenbeſtaendigkeit," Bd. ii. Stuttgart & Tübingen,1850; and in "Grimm," Deutſche Sagen, Bd. ii. Berlin, 1818, p. 186; "Kaiſer Heinrich verſucht die Kaiſerin."

[4] *delyteth*] Orig. reads delyteh.

4 A HUNDRED

The following are more or lefs exact imitations of thefe different fources: Henr. Bebelii "Facetiæ, additamenta Hermotimi," in Nicod. Frifchlini "Facet. Selectiores," Amftelod. 1660, p. 313; Joh. Gaftius, "Convivalium fermonum," Bafil, 1549, tom. i. p. 198; Ser Giovanni Fiorentino, "Il Pecorone," giorn. iii. nov. 2; Celio Malefpini, "Ducento novelle," nov. 61; Ludov. Domenichi, "Facetie," p. 204; Matteo Bandello, "Novelle," tom. ii. nov. 25; "Conti da ridere," tom. i. p. 139 "d'un uomo che fu cornuto, battuto e contento;" Timoneda, "Alivio de Caminantes," p. i. No. 69, reprinted in "Bibl. de Aut. Efpañ." vol. iii. p. 175; "Romanzero general," Madrid, 1614, p. ix. fol. 344; H. Eftienne (Henr. Stephanus) "Apologie pour Hérodote, augm. de remarques par Le Duchat," La Haye, 1735, tom. i. chap. 15, p. 279; Dancourt, "Oeuvres," Paris, 1729; tom. ii. No. 1, "Le tuteur;" "Roger Bontems en belle humeur," Cologne, 1731, tom. i. p. 55: "D'un homme qui fut cocu, battu et content;" "Contes à rire, ou Récréations Françaifes," ed. 1787, tom. ii. p. 130; Lafontaine, Contes: "Le Cocu battu et content," liv. i. c. 3; B. Waldis, "Efopus," iv. 81; Joh. Pet. de Memel, "Luftige Gefellfchaft" (imperfect copy of the Library in Göttingen), No. 2, f. 26; Philander, "Der Kurzweilige Zeitverkürzer," s. l. 1702, No. 481, p. 323; A. F. E. Langbein, Schwänke: "Der Kammerdiener," ed. 1765, Bd. i. p. 29; "A Sackful of Newes," London, 1673, reprinted in Mr. Hazlitt's "Shakefpeare Jeft-Books," 2nd feries, Lond. 1864, p. 169.

WYFE ther was which had apointed her prētys to com to her bed in the night which feruāt had long woyd her to haue his plefure which acordīge to the apoītmēt

MERY TALYS.

cã to her bed ſyde ĩ the night her huſbãd liyng by her & when ſhe pceyuyd hym ther ſhe caught hĩ by the hãd & hyld hym faſt & incõtinẽt wakened her huſbõd & ſayd/ Sir it is ſo ye haue a fals & an vntru feruãt to you which is william your prentys & has lõge woyd me to haue his pleſur/ & becawſe I coud nat auoyde his importunate requeſt I haue appoĩtyd hym this night to met me in the gardẽ ĩ the herber & yf ye wyll aray your ſelf in myn aray & go theder ye ſhall ſe the ȝpfe therof & then ye may rebuke hym as ye thĩke beſt by your dyſcrecyon/ this huſbãd thus aduertiſed by his wyfe/ put vpõ hym his wyues raymẽt¹ & went to the herber and when he was gone thyder the prentys cã in to bed to his maſtres wher for a ſeaſõ they wer both contẽt and pleaſyd ech other by the ſpace of an hour or .ij. but when ſhe thought tyme cõuenyẽt ſhe ſayd to the prentyſe Now go thy way in to the herber & mete hym & take a good waſter² in thy hãd & ſay thou dydys it but to ȝpue whether I woldbe a good womã or no & reward hym as thou thynkyſt beſt. This prentys doĩg after his maſtres cõcell wẽt to³ the herber wher he founde his maſter ĩ his maſtres appel & ſayd A thou

---

¹ *rayment*] Orig. reads raymtẽ.
² *waſter*] i.e. cudgel.
³ *went to*] Hazl. went in to.

harlot art thou comē hether/ now I ſe well yf I wold be fals to my maſter thou woldeſt be a ſtrōg hore but I had leuer thou wer hāgyd thā I wold do him ſo traterous a dede therfore I ſhall gyve the ſome puniſhment as thou lyke an hore haſt deſeruyd/ & therwith lapt hī well about the ſholds & bak and gaue hym a doſē or .ii. good ſtrypys the maſter felyng hym ſelfe sōwhat to ſmart ſayd peſe wylliā myne own true good ſeruāt for godys ſake hold thy hādys for I ā thi maſter & not thi maſtres/ na hore quod he thou lyeſt thou art but an harlot & I dyd but to pue the/ & ſmote hī agayn. Alas man quod the maſter I beſeche the nomore for I am not ſhe for I am thy maſter fele for I haue a berd/ and therwith he ſparyd his hād & felt hys berd. Alas maſter[1] quod the prentys I crye you mercy & then the mayſter went vnto hys wyfe & ſhe aſkyd hym how he had ſped & he āſwerd I wis[2] wyfe I haue bene ſhrewdly betyn how be it I haue cauſe to be glad for I thanke god I haue as trew a wyfe & as trew a ſeruant as any man hath in englond.

⁋ By this tale ye may ſe that it is not wyſdome for a man to be rulyd alway after hys wyues councell.

[1] *Alas maſter*] Hazl. good mayſter.
[2] *I wis*] i. e. I know.

MERY TALYS.

IV. *Of hym that playd the deuyll and came thorow the waren & mayd theym that ſtale the connys to ronne away.*

T fortunyd that in a market towne in the counte of Suffolk there was a ſtage play ĩ the which playe on callyd Johñ adroyns wich dwelyd ĩ a nother vyllage ij. myle frõ thẽs playd the deuyll. And whẽ the play was done this Johñ adroyns ĩ the euenyng departyd fro the ſayd market towne to go home to his owne houſe & be cauſe³ he had there no chãge of clothĩge he went forth ĩ his deuylls apell whiche ĩ the way comyng homward cã thorow a waren of conys belõgyng to a gẽtylmã of the vyllage wher he hym ſelfe dwelt. at which tyme it fortunyd a preſt a vycar of a church therby with ij. or iij. other vnthryfty felowes had brought with thẽ a hors a hey & a feret to thẽtẽt ther to get conis & whẽ the feret was in the yerth & the hey⁴ ſet ouer the path way wherĩ⁵ thys Johñ adroyns ſhold com. this preſt & this⁶ other felowes ſaw hym com ĩ the deuyls raymẽt cõſyderĩg that they were ĩ the deuyls ſeruyſe & ſtelĩg of cones & ſuppoſynge it had ben the deuyll in dede for

---

³ *& be cauſe*] Hazl. becauſe.   ⁴ *a hey*] i. e. a net.
⁵ *wherin*] Hazl. where.   ⁶ *& this*] Hazl. and his.

fere ran away. this John adroyns ĩ the deuyls raymẽt & be caufe it was fõwhat dark faw not the hey but wẽt forth ĩ haft & ftõblid therat & fell down & wyth¹ the fall he had almoft broke his nek.²

But whẽ he was a lytyll reuyuyd he lokyd vp & fpyed it was a hay to chach connys & lokyd further/ & faw that they ran away for fere of hym/ & faw a horfe tyed to a bufh laden with connys whych they had taken/ & he toke the horfe & the haye & lepe³ vpõ the horfe & rode to the gentylmannys place that was lorde of the waren/ to the entente to haue thanke for takynge fuche a pray. And when he cam/ knokyd at the gatys. To whome anone one of gentylmannys feruauntys afkyd who was there/ and fodeynly openyd the gate/ and affone as he perceyuyd hym in the deuyls raymente was fodenly abafhyd/ and fparryd the dore agayn/ & went in to his mayf-ter/ and fayd & fware to hys mayfter that the deuyll was at the gate/ and wolde come in. The gentylman heryng hym fay fo callyd another of hys feruaũntys & bad hym go to the gate to knowe who was there. This feconde feruaũt

---

        & wyth   Hazl. that with.
[2] The words *his nek* in orig. accidentally are omitted.
[3] *lepe*] Hazl. lept.

cam to the gate durſt not open it/ but aſkyd with lowd voyce who was there. thys Johñ Adroyns[4] in the deuyls apperell anſwerd with a hye voyce and ſayd/ Tell thy maſter I muſt nedys ſpeke with hym or[5] I go. This fecõd feruaũt heryng that anſwer ſuppoſynge alſo it had bene the deuyll/ went in agayn to his maſter and ſayd thus/ mayſter yt is the deuyll in dede that ys at the gate/ and ſayth he muſt nedys ſpeke with you or he go hens. The gentylmã then began a lyttvll to baſhe and callyd the ſteward of hys howſe/ whyche was the wyſyſt feruaunt that he had and bad hym to go to the gate and to brynge hym ſure worde who was there. This ſteward be cauſe he thaught he wold ſe ſurely who was there came to the gate and lokyd thorow the chinys of the gate in dyuers placys/ and ſaw well that yt was the deuyll and ſat vpon an horſe and hang-ynge aboute the ſaddell on euery ſyde ſawe the cony heddys hengynge down/ than he came to his mayſter aferde in greate haſte and ſayd/ By goddys body yt is the deuyll in dede that is at the gate ſyttyng vpon an horſe laden all wyth fowllys/ and by lykelyhede/[6] he is com for your

---

[4] *Adroyns*] Orig. reads Androyns.
[5] *or*] i. e. ere, before.
[6] *by lykelyhede*] Hazl. be lykelyhode.

foule¹ purpofely/ and lakkyth but your foule/ &
yf he had your fowle I wene² he fhold be gone.
This gentylman thã merueloufly abafhyd callyd
vp³ his chapleyn/ and made the holy candell to be
lyght/ and gat holy water and wente to the gate
wyth as many of hys feruauntys as durfte go with
hym/ where the chaplayn with holy wordys of
coniuracyon fayde/ In the name of the fader/
fonne and holy gooft/ I coniure the and charg
the in the holy name of god to tell me why and
wherfore thowe commyfte hyther.

This Johñ Androynys in the deuyllys apparell
heryng theym begynne to cõiure after fuche maner
fayd/ Nay nay be not a ferd of me for I am a good
dyuell I am Johñ Adroyns your neghboour dwellyng in thys towne⁴ and he that played the dyuell/
to day in the play/ I haue braught my mayfter a
dofen or ii.⁵ of hys owne connyes that were ftolyn
in hys waren and theyr horfe & theyr hay/ and
made theym for fere to ronne away/ and when
they⁶ herde hym thus fpeke by hys voyce they
knew hym well ynoughe⁷ and openyd the gate

¹ *foule*] in orig. fonle.   ² *I wene*] I fuppofe.
³ *callyd vp*] Hazl. called.
⁴ *dwellyng in thys towne*] Hazl. in this towne.
⁵ *ii.*] Hazl. two.
⁶ *and when they*] Hazl. whanne they.
⁷ *they knew hym well ynoughe*] Hazl. knewe him well.

and let hym come in/ And fo all the forfayd fere and dred[8] was tornyd to myrth and dyfporte.

¶ By this tale ye may fe that mẽ fear many tymes more than they nede which hath caufyd mẽ to beleue that fpyryttys & deuyls haue bene fene in dyuers placys when it hath bene nothynge fo.

v. *Of the fyk man that bequethyd hys thyrd fon a lytyll ground with the galows.*

THER was a riche man which lay fore feke in his bed lyke to dy[9] wherfore his eldyſt fon cam to hym & befechyd hym to gyue hym his blyſſyng to whom the fader fayd fon thou ſhalt haue goddys bleſſyng & myne and for that that[10] thou haſt ben euer good of cõdycyons I gyue & bequeth the all my land/ to whom he anfwered & fayd nay faḋ I truſt you ſhal lyue & occupy them your felfe full well by goddys grace. Sone after came his ij. fone[11] to hym lyke wyfe & defyred his bleſſyng/ to whom the faḋ fayd becaufe[12] thou haſt be[13] euer kynde

[8] *fere and dred*] Hazl. feare.
[9] *lyke to dy*] Hazl. to (deth).
[10] *for that that*] Hazl. becaufe.
[11] *his ij. fone*] Hazl. another fonne.
[12] *becaufe*] Hazl. my fonne.   [13] *be*] Hazl. ben.

& gentyll[1] & I geue the goddys bleſſynge & myn and alſo[2] I bequeth the all my mouable goodys/ to whom he anſwerd and ſayd/ nay fader I truſt ye ſhall lyve & do well & ſpend and vſe your goodys your ſelfe by goddys grace. Anon after the iij. ſone cam to hym & deſyred his bleſſyng to whom the fader anſwerd & ſayd by cauſe thou haſt bene euyll & ſtoborne of condycyons & wolde neuer be ruled after my coūſell I haue nother land nor goodys onbequethyd but onely a lytell vacant ground wher a galows ſtandyth which now I geue and bequeth to the/ and goddys curſe withall/ to whom the ſonne anſwerd as hys bretherne dyd & ſayd nay fader I truſt ye ſhall lyue and be in good helth and haue yt and occupy it your ſelfe by goddys grace. But after that the fader dyed & this thyrd ſon cōtynuyd ſtyll hys vnthryfty condycyons wherefore yt was hys fortune afterwarde for hys deſeruyng to be hangyd on the ſame galows.

¶ By this tale men may wel perceyue that yong people that wyll not be rulyd by theyr frendys councell in youth in tymys come to a ſhamfull ende.

[1] *gentyll &*] Hazl. gentyll.
[2] *and alſo*] Hazl. and.

VI. *Of the gentylman that loſt his ryng in the gentylwomans bed, & a nother gentylman found it after in the ſame bed.*

This tale is taken from the " Cent Nouvelles Nouvelles," nouv. 62. It is imitated by Celio Maleſpini in " Ducento novelle," nov. 2, and by Decker and Webſter in " Northward Hoe," 160 f, act. 1, ſc. i. See Webſter's Works, ed. by *A. Dyce.* London, 1830, vol. iii. p. 139.

TWO gẽtylmen of accoyntaũce wer appoyntyd to ly with a gẽtyll[3] womã in one nyght[4] the one not knowĩge of the other at dyuers tymis. This fyrſt at[5] his houre appoyntyd cã/ & in the bed ther he fortunid to leſe a ryng/ the .ij.[6] gentylmã when he was gone cam/ & fortunyd to fynd the ſame rynge/ & when he had ſped hys beſynes departyd/ & .ij. or .iij.[7] dayes after the furſt gẽtylman ſeyng hys ryng on the others fynger chalengyd yt[8] of hym & he[9] denyed yt hym & bad hĩ tell wher he had loſt it & he ſeyd ĩ ſuch a gentylwomans

---
[3] *gẽtyll*] Orig. reads gẽyll.
[4] *in one nyght*] Hazl. both in one nyght.
[5] *at*] Orig. reads ad.
[6] *the ij.*] Hazl. the ſeconde.
[7] *ij. or iij.*] Hazl. two or thre.
[8] *chalengyd yt*] Hazl. and chalenged it.
[9] *& he*] Orig. reads he &.

bed/ than quod the other & ther founde I yt/ & the one fayd he wolde haue yt/ the other fayd he fhulde not/ thã they agreyd to be iuggid by the next mã that they mote/¹ & it fortunid theym to mete with the hufbãd of the fayd gentyll womã & defyryd hym of his beft Jugemēt fhowyng hym all hole² mater/ then quod he by my iugemēt he that owd³ the fhetys fhould haue the ryng/ thē quod they & for your good iugemēt you fhall haue the ryng.

VII. *Of the hufband man that afkyd for mafter pyfpot the phyfyfyõ.*

Wanting in Hazl. B. Waldis, "Efopus," iv. 23. In Jafander, " Der Teutfche Hiftorien Schreiber," Frankf. et Leipz. 1730, No. 128, p. 246, a fimilar ftory is related: a peafant afks for Dr. Lindwurm (Dragon) inftead of Dr. Drachen, &c. Jt. No. 27; Jt. Taylor, "Wit and Mirth," p. 101.

N a vyllage in fuffex there dwellyd a hufbandmã whofe wyfe fortunyd to fall fyk. Thys hufbandman came to the preeft of the church and defyryd hys councell

---

¹ *mote*] Hazl. dyd mete.
² *all hole*] Hazl. all the hole.
³ *owd*] Hazl. ought.

what thyng was beſt to help his wyfe/ whych anſweryd hym & ſayd y^t in bredſtrete in londõ there was a connyng Pheſycyon whoſe name is callyd maſter Jordayne/ Go to hym & ſhew hym that thy wyfe is ſyk and Jmpotent & not able to go & ſhew hym her water and beſeech hym to be good maſter to the/ and praye hym to do hys cure vppon her: and I warrant he wyll tech the ſome medſyne that ſhall help her. Thys huſbandman folowyng hys councell cã to london & aſkyd of dyuers men which was the way to good ale ſtrete[4] ſo y^t euery man y^t hard hym laught hym to ſcorne. At the laſt on y^t harde hym aſkyd him whether it were not bred ſtrete that he wold haue/ By god quod the huſbandmã ye ſay treuth: for I wyſt well it was other brede or drink: So whẽ they had taught hym the way to bred ſtrete & was ēteryd into y^e ſtrete he aſkyd of dyuers men where one maſter Pyſpot dwellyd whych ſayd they knew no ſuch mã & laught at hym apace. At laſt one aſkyd him whether it were not maſter Jordayn ye phyſyciõ. ye y^e ſame quod ye huſbandmã for I wot well a iordayn & a pyſpot is all one. So whẽ they had ſhewyd hym hys houſe he wẽt thyder & cã to hym & dyd hys erãd thys & ſayd/ Syr if it

---

[4] *ſtrete*] Orig. reads ſtrere.

pleafe your mafhyp I vnderftand ye ar callyd a conyng confufyon: So it is my wyfe is fyk & omnypotent & may not go & here Ihaue brought you her water I befech you do your corage vppon her & I fhall gyue your mafhyp a good reward. The phefyciõ pfeyṅyng by the water y^t fhe was weke of nature bad hym get her mete y^t were reftoratyue & fpecyally if he coud let her haue a poũdgarnet & to let her not ouercome her ftomak w^t mych mete tyll fhe haue an apetyte. Thys hufbãdmã herd him fpeke of a poundgarnet & an apetite had wend he had fpoken of a pound of garlyk and of an ape & fhortly bought a pound of garlyk & after went to the ftylyard & bought an ape of one of the marchantys & brought both home to hys wyfe and tyed the ape w^t a cheyn at hys beddys fete/ & made hys wyfe to ete the pound of garlyk whether fhe wolde or no/ whereby fhe fell in fo great a lafk that it purgyd all the corrupciõ out of her body: whereby & by refõ y^t the ape that was tyde ther made fo many mokkys fkyppys & knakkys that made her oftymys to be mery & laugh that thankyd be god fhe was fhortly reftoryd to helth.

¶ By thys tale ye may fe that oft tymys medefyns taken at aduenturys do as mich good to the Pacyent as medefyns geuen by the folempne coũcell of conyng phyfycyons.

VIII. *Of the ſcoler that bare his ſhoys to cloutyng.*

A ſimilar affectation in " Neuvermehrte luſtige Pennal-Poſſen," s. l. & a. 8vo. ſign. E. 6.

IN the vnyuerſyte of Oxonford there was a ſkoler y^t delytyd mich to ſpeke eloquent engliſh & curious termis/ And cã to ye cobler wyth hys ſhoys whych were pikid before as they vſyd y^t ſeſon[1] to haue them cloutyd & ſayd thys wyſe/ Cobler I pray the ſet me .ii. tryangyls & .ii.[2] ſemy cercles vppon my ſubpedytals & I ſhall gyue the for thy labor/ This cobler[3] becauſe he vnderſtode hym not half well[4] ãſwerid ſhortly & ſayd/ Syr youre eloquence paſſith myne ĩtelligence/ but I promyſe you yf ye[5] meddyll wyth me/ the clowtyng of your ſhone ſhall coſte you .iij.[6] pence.

¶ By thys tale mẽ may lerne y^t it is foly to ſtudy to ſpeke eloquẽtly before them that be rude & vnlernyd.

[1] *as they vſyd that ſeſon*] Hazl. (as they uſed that tyme).
[2] *ij*] Hazl. two.
[3] *This cobler*] Hazl. The cobeler.
[4] *half well*] Hazl. halfe.
[5] *ye*] Hazl. he.
[6] *iij*] Hazl. thre.

IX. *Of him that sayd that a womās tong was lightift met of degeftiō.*

The fource of this tale is Johannes de Bromyard, "Summa prædicantium," s. l. & a. fol. Litt. L. v. § 21, Exempl. i.: "Patet per hiftoriam qua fertur infirmum refpondiffe medico dicenti: quod comederet de parte pifcium caude propinquiori: quia fanior erat pars: quia plus mouebatur: ergo inquit infirmus: lingua uxoris mee faniffima eft, quia continue mouetur." Reprinted from a MS. in the Britifh Mufeum in Th. Wright, "Latin Stories from MSS. of the 13th and 14th Centuries," London, 1842; (Percy Society, vol. viii.), No. 132: "De Linguis Mulierum."

Another verfion is found in Vincentii Bellovacenfis, "Speculum Morale," Duaci, 1624, fol. 86: "Narratvr de quodam, quod cum ipfe in mari haberet vxorem fuam fecum lingualam, grauem ad tolerandum: cum imminente tempeftate clamatum effet a nautis, quod grauiora de naui proiicerentur, ille exhibuit vxorem dicens quod in tota naui non erat aliquid grauius lingua eius." It is imitated in H. Bebelii, "Facetiæ, opufcula," s. l. & a. (circa 1512), 4°. fign. Cc, verfo: "De quodam in tempeftate maris deprehenfo (de alio)," and repeated in Joh. Gaftius, "Convivalium Sermonum," tom. i. p. 281, Bafil, 1549.

CERTAYN artificer in londō there was which was fore fyk that coud not well dygeft hys mete/ to whō a phyfycō cam to gyue hym councell & feyd y^t he muft vfe to ete metis y^t be light of dygeftyon as

small byrdys/[1] as sparous or swallous & especyall[2] yt byrd yt ys callyd a wagtale whose fleshe ys merueloufe lyght of dygestyõ becaufe that byrd ys euer mouyng & styryng. The sik man heryng the pheficion seyd so answeryd hym & seyd/ Syr yf that be the caufe yt thofe birdys be lyght of dygestyon/ Than I know a mete mych lyghter of dygestion thã other sparow swallow or wagtayle/ & that ys my wyuys tõg for it is neuer in rest but euer mouying & styrryng.

¶ By thys tale ye may lerne a good generall rule of phefyk.

x. *Of the woman that folowyd her fourth husbandys herce & wept.*

WOMAN ther was whych had had .iiii. husbãdes. It fortunyd alfo that this fourth hufband died & was brought to chirch vppon ye bere/ whõ this womã folowyd & made gret mone & wext very fory. In fo mych that her neybours thought she wold fowne & dy for forow/ wherfor one of her goffyps cam to her & spake to her in her ere &

[1] *as small byrdys*] Hazl. and small byrdys.
[2] *efpecyall*] Hazl. efpecyally.

bad her for goddes fake to comfort[1] her felf &
refrayne that lamentacõn or ellys it wold hurt
her gretly[2] & pauenture put her in ieoperdy of
her lyfe. To whõ this womã ãfweryd & fayd/
I wys good gofyp I haue gret caufe to morne if
ye knew all/ for I haue byryed .iii. hufbandys be-
fyde thys man/ but I was neuer ĩ the cafe y^t I am
now/ for there was not one of thē but whē that
I folowid the corfe to chyrch yet I was fure
alway[3] of an other hufbãd before that ye corfe[4]
cam out of my houfe/ & now I am fure of no
nother hufband & therfore ye may be fure I haue
gret caufe to be fad and heuy.

¶ By thys tale ye may fe that the olde puerbe
ys trew that yt is as gret pyte to fe a woman wepe
as a gofe to go barefote.

XI. *Of the woman that fayd her wooer came
to late.*

This tale is taken from H. Bebelii, "Facetiæ, opufcula,"
s. l. & a. 4º. fign. Ggii : " De quadam muliere citiffime nu-
bente poft obitum primi viri : quidam caupo erat ad pontem
æni; vulgo Ifbruck, qui cum ad medium annum valetudinarius

[1] *to comfort*] Hazl. comfort.
[2] *hurt her gretly*] Hazl. hurt her.
[3] *I was fure alway*] Hazl. I was fure.
[4] *before that the corfe*] Hazl. before the corfe.

vitam tandem cum morte commutaffet, vxor eius funus profecuta miferabiles edebat eiulatus, obftinateque lachrymabat, adeo vt ducere eam cogeretur feruus fuus, qui eam pro virili parte confolabatur. Cum vero ipfa quereretur fe neminem habere cum quo cauponam adminiftraret (vt moris eft mulieribus multa conquerentibus) famulus fua in homines merita, qualiter quoque notus effet declarando, appellauit eam de coniugio. Illa inter eiulandum dixit. Ah nimis fero petifti, paulo enim ante alteri promifi."

Imitated in "Uncafing of Machivils Inftructions to his Sonne," 1613, fign. C, 3, and in J. W. Kirchhof, "Wendunmuth," Frankf. 1573, i. No. 346, fol. 333. Joh. Pet. de Memel, "Luftige Gefellfchaft," ed. 1695, No. 524, goes even farther, the wife was already engaged before the death of her hufband.

NOTHER woman there was that knelyd at ye mas of requiẽ whyle the corfe of her hufbande lay on the bere in the chyrch. To whom a yonge man came to fpeke wyth her in her ere as thoughe hyt had bene for fom matre concernyng the funerallys/howe be yt he fpake of no fuch matter but only wowyd her that he myghte be her hufbande/to whome fhe anfwerye & fayde thus/ Syr by my trouthe I am fory that ye come fo late/ for I am fped all redy/ For I was made fure yefter day to a nother man.

¶ By thys tale ye may perceyue that women ofte tymes be wyfe and lothe to lofe any tyme.

XII. *Of the mylner with the golden thombe.*

See Brand's "Popular Antiquities," 1849, vol. iii. p. 387; Hazlitt's edition, p. 23, note 2, and p. 125, note to p. 23.

MERCHANT that thought to deride a myllner ſeyd vnto yᵉ mylner ſyttyng among company. Sir I haue hard ſay that euery trew mylner that tollythe trewlye hath a gyldeyn thombe/ the mylner anſwered & ſeyd it was trewth/[1] Then quod the merchaunt I pray the let me ſe thy thomb/ & when the mylner ſhewyd hys thomb the merchaunt ſayd I can not perceyue yᵗ thy thombe is gylt/ but yt ys but[2] as all other mennys thõbis be/to whom the mylner anſweryd & ſeyd/ Syr trothe yt ys that my thõb is gylt how be it[3] ye haue no power to ſe it/ for ther is a properte euer incidēt therto yᵗ he yᵗ ys a cokecold ſhall neuer haue power to ſe yt.

XIII. *Of the horſman of yrelond that prayd Oconer to hang vp the frere.*

A very ſimilar ſtory in "Neuvermehrte luſtige Pennal-Poſſen," s. l. & a. 8vo. ſign. C, 5 *verſo;* and in Jacob Frey,

---

[1] *trewth*] Hazl. true.   [2] *but it is but*] Hazl. but it is.
[3] *how be it*] Hazl. but.

"Die Gartengesellschaft," s. l. & a. (1556), Cap. 125, fol. 122: "Einen Dieb wolt man henken, der bat den Pfarrherrn, er solt das Nachtmahl für ihn essen," ed. Frankf. 1590, fol. 97.

ONE callyd[4] Oconer an yrish lorde toke an horseman pryfoner that was one of hys gret enmys/ whiche for any requeſt or yntrety y^t ye horſman made gaue iugement that he ſhulde incõtynēt be hãgyd/ & made a frere to ſhryue hym and bad hym make hym redy to dye. Thys frere y^t ſhroue hym examyned hym of dyuers ſynes & aſkyd hym amõg othere whyche were the grettyſte ſynnys that euer he dyde/ thys horſeman anſweryd & ſayde one of the grettyſt actys that euer I dyde whyche I now moſt repent is that when I toke Oconer the laſte weke in a churche and ther I myght haue brennyd hym church and all & becauſe I had confcyence & pyte of brennyng of the church I taryed ye tyme ſo long y^t oconer eſcaped/ & that ſame deferring of brennyng of the church & ſo long taryeng of that tyme is one of the worſt actys y^t euer I dyd wherof I moſte repente/ Thys frere perceyuyng hym in that mynd ſayd pece man[5] in the name of god & change y^t mynde

[4] *One callyd*] Hazl. One whiche was called.
[5] *pece man*] Hazl. peace.

& dye in charite or els thou ſhalt neuer come in heuen/ nay quod the hors man I wyll neuer change yᵗ mynde what ſo euer ſhall come to my ſoule/ thys frere ꝑceyuyng hym thys ſtyll to contynew hys mĩde cã to oconer & ſeyd ſyr in yᵉ name of god haue ſome pyte vppõ thys mannys ſowle & let hym not dye now tyll he be in a better mynde/ For yf he dye now he ys ſo far out of charyte yᵗ vtterly hys ſoule ſhalle be dampnyd/ and ſhewyd hym what mynde he was in & all the hole matter as ys before ſhewyd. Thys horſman heryng yᵉ frere thys intrete for hym ſayd to oconer thys/ Oconer thou ſeeyſt well by thys mannys reporte yᵗ yf I dye now I am out of charyte & not redy to go to heuen & ſo it ys yᵗ I am now out of charyte in dede/ but thou ſeeſt well yᵗ this frere ys a good man he is now¹ well dyſpoſyd & in charyte/ and he is redy to go to heuen & ſo am not I/ therfore I pray the hang vp thys frere whyle that he hys redy to go to heuyn and lette me tary tyl a nother tyme yᵗ I may be ĩ charyte and redy & mete to go to heuyn. This Oconer heryng this mad anſwere of hym ſparyd the man & forgaue hym hys lyfe at that ſeaſon.

¶ By thys ye may ſe that he that is in daunger of his enmye yᵗ hath no pyte/ he can do no better

---

¹ *he is now*] Hazl. and he is now.

than² fhew to hym the vttermofte of hys ma-
lycyous mynde whych that he beryth toward
hym.

xiv. *Of the preft that fayd nother corpus meus nor corpum meum.*

THE archdekyn of Effex yᵗ had bene long in auctoryte in a tyme of vyfytacion when all the preeftys apperyd before hym callyd afyde .iii. of yᵉ yõg preftys whych were accufyd yᵗ they coud not well fay theyr deuyne feruyce/ & afkyd of thẽ whẽ they fayd mas whether they fayd corpus meus or corpũ meũ. The furft preeft fayd yᵗ he fayd corpus meus. The fecõd fayd yᵗ he fayd corpũ meũ. And thẽ he afkyd of the thyrd how he fayd/ whych anfweryd & fayd thus/ fyr becaufe it is fo gret a dout & dyuers men be in dyuers opynyons/ therfore becaufe I wold be fure I wold not offend whẽ I come to yᵉ place I leue it clene out & fay no-thyng therfore/ wherfore he³ then openly rebukyd them all thre. But dyuers that were prefent thought more defaut in hym becaufe he hym

² *than*] Hazl. but.
³ *wherfore he*] Hazl. wherfore the byfhoppe.

felfe before tyme had admyttyd them to be preeſtys.

¶ By thys tale ye may ſe that one ought to take hede how he rebukyth an other leſt it torne moſt to hys owne rebuke.

xv. *Of the .ii. frerys wherof the one louyd not the ele hed nor the other the tayle.*

TWO frerys ſat at a gentylmans tabyll whych had before hym õ a faſtyng day an ele & cut the hed of the ele & layd it vppõ oneof yᵉ Freres trẽchars/ but the Frere be-cauſe he wold haue had of yᵉ myddyll part of the ele ſayd to the gentylman he louyd no ele heddes/ this gentylman alſo cut the tayle of yᵉ ele & leyd it on the other Freres trẽchar/ he lykewyſe be-cauſe he wold haue had of the myddyll pte of yᵉ ele ſayd he louyd no ele taylys. Thys gentylmã perceyuyng that: gaue the tayle to the Frere[1] yᵗ ſayd he louyd not the hed/ & gaue the hed to hym that ſayd he louyd not yᵉ tayle. And as for the myddell parte of the ele he ete part him ſelf & part he gaue to other folke at yᵉ table/ wherfore theſe freres for anger wold ete neuer a

---

[1] *to the Frere*] Hazl. to hym.

moſſell/ & ſo they for all theyr craft & ſubtylte were not onely deceyued of ye beſt moſſell of ye ele/ but therof had no part at al.

¶ By this ye ſe that they that couet the beſt part ſomtyme therfore loſe the meane part and all.

XVI. *Of the welchmā that ſhroue hym for brekyng his faſt on the fryday.*

This tale is found in Poggii, " Facetiæ, Opera," Baſil, 1538, fol. p. 439: " De quodam paſtore ſimulatim confitente: Paſtor ouium ex ea regni Neapolitani ora, quæ olim latrociniis operam dabant ſemel confeſſorem adijt, ſua peccata dicturus. Cum ad ſacerdotis genua procubuiſſet, parce mihi (inquit ille lachrimans) pater mi, quoniam grauiter deliqui. Cum juberet dicere quid eſſet. Atque ille ſæpius id verbum interaſſet, tanquam qui nepharium admiſiſſet ſalus. Tandem hortatu ſacerdotis, ait ſe cum caſeum faceret, ieiunij tempore, expreſſura lactis guttas quaſdam quas non ſpreuiſſet in os defilijſſe. Tum ſacerdos qui mores illius patriæ noſſet ſubridens, cum dixiſſet illum delinquiſſe qui quadrageſimam non ſeruaſſet, quæſivit numquid aliis obnoxius eſſet peccatis? Abnuente paſtore, rogauit num cum alijs paſtoribus quenquam peregrinum ut mos eſſet illius regionis tranſeuntem ſpoliaſſet, aut peremiſſet? Sæpius inquit, uterque in re cum reliquis ſum verſatus. Sed iſtud ait apud nos ita eſt conſuetum, ut nulla conſcientia fiat," &c.

WELCHMAN dwellynge in a wylde place of walys came to hys curate in the tyme of lent & was cōfeffyd. & when his confeffyon was in maner at the end the curate afked him whether[1] he had any other thyng to fay yᵗ greuyd his cōfcyẽce/ whych fore abafshyd anfweryd no word a gret whyle/ at laft by exortacion of hys gooftly fader he fayd yᵗ there was one thyng in his mynd that gretly greuyd hys cōfciẽce which he was afhamed to vtter/ for it was fo greuous yᵗ he trowid god wold neuer forgyue hym/ to whom the curate ãfweryd & fayd yᵗ goddys mercy was aboue all/ & bad hym not dyfpayre in the mercy of god/ For what fo euer it was yf he were repentaũte yᵗ god wold forgyue hym/ And fo by long exortacion at the laft he fhewyd it & feyd thus/ Syr it happenyd onis that as my wyfe was making a chefe vppon a fryday I wold haue[2] fayed whether it had ben falt or frefh and toke a lytyll of the whey in my hand & put it in my mouth & or I was ware part of it went downe my throte agaynft my wyll & fo I brake my faft/ to whom the curate fayd & if ther be no nother

[1] *whether*] Hazl. and.
[2] *I wold haue*] Hazl. I wolde fayne haue.

thyng I warant god ſhall forgiue the. So whã he had well comfortyd hym wᵗ yᵉ mercy of god the curate prayd hym to anſwer a queſtion & to tell hym treuth/ & when the welchman had promyſyd to tell the treuth/ the curate ſayd that there were robberys and murders done nye the place where he dwelt & dyuers men foũd ſlayne & aſkyd hym whether he were cõſentyng to any of them/ to whõ he anſwerid & ſayd yes & ſayd he was ptee to many of them & dyd helpe to robbe and to ſle³ dyuers of them. Then the curate aſkyd hym why he dyd not cõfeſſe him therof/ the welch man ãſweryd & ſayd he toke yᵗ for no ſynne for it was a cuſtome amonge them yᵗ whan any boty came of any rych merchaunt rydyng yᵗ it was but a good neybours dede one to help a nother when one callyd a nother/ & ſo they toke that but for good felyſhyp & neybourhod.

¶ Here ye may⁴ ſe yᵗ ſome haue remorſe of conſcyence of ſmall venyall ſinys & fere not to do gret offencys wᵗout ſhame of yᵉ world or drede of god : & as yᵉ cõen puerb is they ſtũble at a ſtraw & lepe ouer a blok.

³ *to ſle*] Orig. reads toſle.
⁴ *ye may*] Hazl. maye ye.

xvii. *Of the merchaũt of lõdõ that put nobles ĩ his mouth ĩ his deth bed.*

A RYCH couetous marchãte ther was yᵗ dwellyd in Lõdon whych euer gaderyd money & coud neuer fynd in hys hert to fpend noght¹ vppon hym felf nor vppon no mã els/ whych fell fore fyk/ & as he lay on hys deth bed had hys purs lyeng at his beddys hed/ & had fuche a loue to hys money that he put his hand in his purs & toke out therof .x. or .xii. li ĩ nobles & put them in his mouth/ And becaufe his wyfe and other pceyuyd him very fyk and lyke to dye they exortyd hym to be confeffyd and brought yᵉ curate vnto him/ whych when they had caufyd hym to fey Benedicite yᵉ curat bad hym cry god mercy & fhew his fynnys.² Than this fyk man began to fey I cry god mercy I haue offendyd in yᵉ .vij. dedly fynnys & broken the .x. comaundementys/ & becaufe of the gold in hys mouth he mufflede fo in hys fpeche that the curate cowde not well vnderftande hym/ wherefore the curate afked hym what he hadde in hys mouthe that letted hys fpeche/ I wys maftere perfone quod the fyk man muffelynge

¹ *noght*] Hazl. ought.
² *fhew his fynnys*] Hazl. fhewe to hym.

I haue nothyng in my mouth but a lyttyll money becaufe I wot not whether I fhall go I thoughte I wolde take fome fpendyng money wyth me for I wot not what nede I fhall haue therof/ And incontynent after that feyynge dyed before he was confeffed or repentant that ony man could perceue/ and fo by lykelyhode went to the deuyll.

¶ By thys tale ye may fe that they that all theyre lyuys wylle neuer do charyte to theyr neyghbours/ that god in tyme of theyr dethe wyll not fuffer them to haue grace of repentaunce.

XVIII. *Of the mylner that ftale the nuttys & of the tayler that ftale a fhepe.*

The fource of this tale is perhaps the fabliau Etula, in Legrand d'Auffy, " Fabliaux," tom. iii. p. 77; better in Sinner, " Catalogus Codicum MSS." tom. iii. p. 379, No. 14. It is alfo related in the " Scala Celi (liber ifte vocatur Scala Celi, Ulme, Joh. Zainer, 1480, fol.), de furto, quinto," fol. 101 verfo: " Legitur quod cum duo latrones conveniffent ut furarentur nuces et alter carnes; perveniens ad fores ecclefiæ qui furatus fuerat nuces incepit frangere et comedere eas ibi. Cujus fonitum audiens ille, qui cuftodiebat ecclefiam, credens, quod dæmon ingreffus eft clauftrum et cuidam claudo, qui ire non potuit et forti ruſtico videnti nunciavit. Et dum ingreſſi fuiſſent eccleſiam, latro comedebat nuces, credens quod eſſet ſocius ſuus, qui portaret arietem, incepit clamare: Eſtne bene pinguis quem portas? Tunc ruſticus territus qui portabat claudum, credens quod eſſet dæmon: Neſcio ſi eſt pinguis vel macer, ſed nunc relinquo eum vobis. Et projecto claudo ad terram tibiam aliam ſibi frigit." Alſo in Joh. de Bromyard, "Summa prædicantium," Litt. O, ii. § 6.

Imitations are: J. Pauli, "Schimpff und Ernſt," Straſſburg, 1535, fol. No. 76, fol. 15; G. Wickram, "Der Rollwagen," s. l. 1557, No. 67, (Frankf. 1590, fol. 72: "Wie zween Dieb einem Pfaffen das Podagram vertriben"), reprinted in Wackernagel, "Deutſches Leſebuch," Wickram; Hans Sachs, "Gedichte," vol. ii. l. 4, fol. 73, Nürnberg, 1591, fol.: "Die zwen diebiſchen Bachanten in dem Toden Kercker."

THERE was a certayn ryche huſbandman in a vyllage whych loued nottes merueloufly well & ſet trees of filberdys & other nut trees in his orchard/ & noriſhid them well all hys lyfe/ & when he dyed he made hys executours to make promiſe to bery w^t hym yn hys graue a bage of nottis or els they ſholde not be hys executours/ which executours for fere of loſyng theyre¹ romys fulfyllyd hys wyll² & dyd ſo. It happenyd y^t the ſame nyght after that he was beryed there was a mylnere in a

---

¹ *of loſyng theyre*] Hazl. of leſynge of theyre.
² *wyll*] Hazl. mynde.

MERY TALYS. 33

whyte cote came to this mãys garden to thētēt³ to ſtele a bag of nottis/ & in yᵉ way he met wᵗ a tayler in a blak cote an vnthrift of hys accoyntaũce & ſhewyd hym hys intent/ This tayler lykewyſe ſhewyd hym yᵗ he intēdyd yᵉ ſame tyme to ſtele a ſhepe/ & ſo they both there agreyd to go forthward euery man ſeuerally wᵗ hys purpoſe & after yᵗ they apoynted to make good chere ech wᵗ other & to mete agayne in yᵉ chyrch porch/ & he that came furſt to tary for the other.

This mylner when he had ſpede of hys nottis came furſt to the chyrch porche & there taryed for hys felowe and the mene whyle ſatte ſtyll there & knakked nottys.

It fortuned than the ſexten of the church becauſe yt was abowt .ix. of the clok cam to ryng curfu.⁴ & when he lokyd in yᵉ porch & ſaw one all in whyte knakkyng nottes/ he had went⁵ it had bene yᵉ dede man ryſen owt of hys graue knakkynge yᵉ nottes yᵗ wer byryed wᵗ hym & ran home agayn in all haſt and tolde to a krepyll yᵗ was in hys howſe what he had ſene. This crepyll thus heryng⁶ rebukyd yᵉ ſexten & ſeyd yᵗ

---

³ *to thentent*] i. e. to the entent.
⁴ *curſu*] i. e. evening-bell.
⁵ *went*] i. e. weened.
⁶ *thus heryng*] Hazl. thus herynge hym.

D

yf he were able to go he wold go thyder & cõiure yᵉ fprite/ by my trouth quod yᵉ fexten & yf thou darft do yᵗ I wyl bere the on my nek & fo they both agreed. The fexten toke yᵉ crepul on hys nek & cam in to yᵉ chyrchyard agayn/ & yᵉ mylner in yᵉ porch faw one comyng bering a thing on his bak had went it had ben yᵉ taylour cõmyng wᵗ the fhepe & rofe vp to mete thẽ/ & as he cam towarde thẽ he afkeyd & feyd/ Is he fat/ is he fat/ yᵉ fexten heryng hym fey fo/ for fere caft the crepull down & feyd fat or lene take hym ther for me/¹ and ran away/ & the creple by myracle was made hole & rã away as faft as he or fafter/ This mylner perceyuing yᵗ they were .ii.² & yᵗ one ran after a nother fuppofyng³ yᵗ one had fpyed yᵉ tayler ftelyng yᵉ fhepe & yᵗ he had ron after hym to haue taken hym/ and fered yᵗ fom body alfo had fpyed hym ftelyng nottes⁴ he for fere left hys nottes behynd hym and as fecretly as he cowde ran home to hys myll/ And anon after yᵗ he was gon yᵉ tayler cam wᵗ the ftolyn fhepe vppon hys nek to the chyrch porch⁵ to

---

¹ *ther for me*] Hazl. as he is.
² *.ii.*] Hazl. two.   ³ *fuppofyng*] Hazl. thoughte.
⁴ *and fered that fom body alfo had fpyed hym ftelyng nottes*] Hazl. and fearyng that one had fpyed hym alfo ftelynge the nuttes.
⁵ *chyrch porch*] Hazl. churche.

feke the mylner & when he fownd ther the not
fhalys he fuppofyd yᵗ hys felow had be ther and
gone home as he was in dede/ wherefore he toke
vp yᵉ fhepe agayne on hys nek and went⁶ to
ward the myl/ But yet duryng this whyle the
fextē which ran away went not to hys owne
houfe but wēt to the pyfh pryftis chāber/ &
fhewd hym how the fpryte of yᵉ man was ryfē
out of hys graue knakkīg nottes as ye haue
hard before/ wherfor yᵉ preft fayd that he wold
go cōiure hym yf the fexten wold go wᵗ hym/
& fo they both agreed/ yᵉ preft dyd on hys furples
& a ftole about hys nek & toke holy water wᵗ
hym and cam wᵗ the fextē toward yᵉ church/ &
as fone as he enteryd in to⁷ yᵉ church yarde, The
tayler wᵗ the whyte fhepe on hys nek intendyng
as I before haue fhewid yow to go down to yᵉ
myll met wᵗ them & had went yᵗ yᵉ preft in hys
furples had ben yᵉ mylner in hys whyte cote/ &
feyd to hym by god I haue hym I haue hym
meanyng by⁸ the fhepe yᵗ he had ftolyn/ the preft
perceyuynge the tayler all in blak & a whyte thyng
on hys nek had went it had ben yᵉ deuyll beryng
away the fpryte of yᵉ dede man yᵗ was beryed
& ran away as fafte as he coud takyng yᵉ way
downe toward the myll/ & yᵉ fexten ronnyng

⁶ *and went*] Hazl. went. ⁷ *in to*] Hazl. in.
⁸ *by*] i. e. thereby.

after hĩ. This tayler feyng one folowyng hĩ had went yᵗ one had folowed the mylner to haue don hym fome hurt & thought he wold folow if nede were to help yᵉ mylner. & went forth tyl he cam to the myll & knokked at yᵉ myldore/ yᵉ mylner beyng wᵗyn afked who was ther yᵉ tayler ãfwerd & faid by god I haue caught one of them & made hĩ fure & tyed hym faft by yᵉ leggys menynge by the fhepe yᵗ he had ftolen & had thẽ on hys nek tyed faft by the leggys.[1] But yᵉ mylner heryng hym fey yᵗ he had hym tyed faft by the leggys had wentᶓ it had bẽ the conftable yᵗ had takẽ the tayler for ftelyng of the fhepe & had tyed him by the leggys/ & ferid yᵗ he had comen to haue taken hym alfo for ftelyng of the nottys/ wherfore the mylner openyd a bak dore & ran away as faft as he coud. The taylour heryng the bak dore openyng wẽt on yᵉ other fyde of yᵉ myll/ & there faw the mylner ronnyng away/ & ftode there a littyll whyle mufyng wᵗ yᵉ fhepe on his nek. Then was the paryfh preeft & the fextẽ ftandyng there vnder the mylhoufe hydyng them for fere & faw the taylour agayn wᵗ yᵉ fhepe on his nek had wend ftyll it had bene the dyuyll wᵗ the fpryt of the dede man on hys nek & for fere ran away/ but becaufe they knew not

[1] *menynge by the fhepe . . . by the leggys.*] Wanting in Hazl.

MERY TALYS.   37

the ground well/ the preeſt lepte into a dyche
almoſt ouer the hed lyke to be drounyd that he
cryed wyth a loud voyce help help. Then the
taylour lokyd about & ſaw the mylner roñe away
& the ſexten a nother way & hard the preeſt cry
help: had wend it had bene the cõſtable w^t a
gret cõpany cryeng for help to take hym & to
bryng hym to pryſon for ſtelyng of y^e ſhepe
wherfore he threw downe the ſhepe & ran away
a nother way as faſte as he coud/ & ſo euery
man was afferd of other wythout cauſe.

¶ By thys ye may ſe well it is foly for any
man to fere a thyng to mych tyll that he ſe ſome
proue or cauſe.

XIX. *Of the .iiii. elemētys where they ſhulde ſone be found.*

A ſubſtantially ſimilar ſtory occurs in " Tre hundrede
udvalgte hiſtorier, &c." 4th edit. Copenh. 1781, p. 198
(a tranſlation of Pauli's " Schimpff und Ernſt "); reprinted
in R. Nyerup, " Almindelig Morſkabs laeſning," Copenh.
1816, p. 254. Alſo in H. Sachs, " Gedichte," buch i.
thiel 3, Nüremberg, 1558, fol. f. 255: " Ein geſprech der
vier Element mit Fraw Warheit."

N ye old world when all thyng coud
ſpeke y^e .iiii. elementys met togeder
for many thyngys whych they had to

do becaufe they muſt medyll alway one with a nother: & had cõmunicaciõ to geder of dyuers matters/ & becaufe they coud not conclude all theyr maters at y^t feafon they appoyntyd to breke comunycacyon for y^t tyme & to mete agayn a nother tyme/ therfore ech one of thẽ ſhewyd to other wher theyre moſt abydyng was & where theyr felows ſhuld fynd them if nede ſhuld requyre: & furſt ye yerth fayd brethern ye know well as for me I am pmanẽt alway & not remouable therfor ye may be fure to haue me alway whan ye lyſt. The water feyd yf ye lyſte to feke me ye ſhalbe fure euer[1] to haue me vnder a toft of grene ruſhys or ellys in a womans eye. The wynde fayd yf ye lyſt to feke me[2] ye ſhalbe fure euer to haue me amonge afpyn leuys or els in a womans tong. Then quod the fyre yf any of you lyſt to feke me: ye ſhall euer[3] be fure to fynd me in a flynt ſtone or els in a womans hart.

¶ By thys tale ye may lerne afwell the propertes of y^e .iiii. elementys as ther properte[4] of a woman.

[1] *euer*] wanting in Hazl.
[2] *to feke me*] Hazl. to fpeke wyth me.
[3] *euer*] wanting in Hazl.
[4] *properte*] Hazl. properte is.

xx. *Of the woman that powryd the potage in the Tuggys male.*

THERE was a iuſtyce but late in yͤ realme of englond called maſter Uauyſour a very homly man & rude of condycions & louyd neuer to ſpẽd mych money/ This maſter Uauyſour rode on a tyme in hys cyrcute in a place of the north cõtrey⁵ where he had agreed wᵗ the ſhyryf for a certayn ſome of money for hys chargys thorowe the ſhyre/ ſo that at euery Inne & lodgyng thys maſter vaueſour payd for hys own coſtys. It fortunyd ſo yᵗ when he cam to a certayn lodgyng he cõmaunded one Torpyn hys ſeruãt to ſe yᵗ he vſed good huſbondry⁶ & to ſaue ſuche thynges as were laft & to cary it wᵗ hym to ſerue hym at the next baytyng. Thys Torpyn doyng hys maſters cõmaũdemẽt toke yͤ brokyn brede brokyn mete & all ſych thĩg yᵗ was laft & put it in hys male/⁷ The wyfe of yͤ houſe pceyuyng yᵗ he toke all ſuche fragmentys & vytayle wᵗ hym yᵗ was laft

---

⁵ *in a place of the north contrey*] Hazl. in the northe contrey.
⁶ *huſbondry*] i. e. economy.
⁷ *in hys mayle*] Hazl. in his mayſters cloth ſak. [Hazl. has *cloth ſak* for *male* throughout the whole tale.]

& put it in hys male/¹ ſhe brought vp yᵗ podege yᵗ was laft ĩ the pot & when torpyn had torned hys bak a lytyll ſyde² ſhe pouryd yᵉ podege in to yᵉ male whych ran vpon hys robe of ſkarlet & other hys garmẽtys & rayed³ them very euyll that they were mych hurt therwᵗ. Thys Torpyn ſodeynly tornyd him & ſaw it/ reuylyd the wyfe therfor & ran to hys maſter & told hym what ſhe had don/ wherfor maſter Uaueſour incõtinẽt callyd yᵉ wyfe & ſeyd to her thus. Thou drab quod he what haſt thou dõ why haſt thou pouryd yᵉ podege in my male & marryd my raymẽt & gere/ O ſyr quod yᵉ wyfe I know well ye ar a iudge of yᵉ realme/ & I perceyue by you: your mĩd is to do ryght & to haue that that is⁴ your owne/ & your mynd is to haue all thyng wᵗ you yᵗ ye haue payd for/ both brokyn brede mete⁵ & other thynges yᵗ is left : & ſo it is reaſon that ye haue/ & therfore becauſe your ſeruant hath taken the brede & the mete⁶ & put it ĩ your male I haue therfore put in your male⁷ the podege yᵗ be laft becauſe ye haue well & truly payd for them

¹ *hys male*] Hazl. the cloth ſake.
² *ſyde*] Hazl. aſyde.   ³ *rayed*] i. e. defiled.
⁴ *that that is*] Hazl. that is.
⁵ *brokyn brede mete*] Hazl. broken mete.
⁶ *the brede and the mete*] Hazl. the broken mete.
⁷ *therfore put in your male*] Hazl. therin put.

for yf⁸ I fhuld kepe ony thyng from you y' ye haue payd for: peraduenture ye wold troble me in the law an other tyme.

¶ Here ye may fe y' he y' playth the nygarde to mych fometyme yt torneth hym to hys owne loffe.

XXI. *Of the weddyd men that cam to heuyn to clayme theyr herytage.*

A correfponding tale in Fernan Caballero, "Elia, ó la Efpaña treinta años ha," Madrid, 1857, page 93. (Tranflated into German by H. Wolf, Paderborn, 1860, p. 116.)

A CERTAYNE weddyd man there was whyche whan he was dede cā to heuen gatys to faynt Peter & fayd he cā to claym his herytage⁹ which he had deferuyd. Saynt Peter afkyd hym what he was/ & he fayd a weddyd mā/ anon Seynt peter openyd yᵉ gatys & bad hym come in¹⁰ & fayd he was worthy to haue hys herytage becaufe he had had much trobyll & was worthy to haue a crowne of glory. Anon after y' there cam a nother man that claymyd

---

⁸ *for yf*] Hazl. Yf.
⁹ *his herytage*] Hazl. hys bad heretage.
¹⁰ *come in*] Hazl. to come in.

heuyn/ & fayd to Seynt Peter he had had .ii. wyuys/ to whom Seynt peter āfweryd and fayd come in for thou art worthy to haue a doble crown of glory/ for thou haft had doble troble/ at ye laft there cam a thyrd[1] claymyng heuen & fayd to Saynt peter that he had had .iii. wyuys & defyryd to come in/ what quod Seynte Peter thou haft bene onys in troble & therof delyueryd/ and then wyllyngly woldyft be trobyld agayn & yet agayn therof delyueryd/ & for all y^t couldeft[2] not beware ye thyrde tyme/ but entereft wyllyngely in trobyll agayne therefore go thy way to hell for thou fhalte neuer come in heuen for thou arte not worthy.

¶ Thys tale is a warnyng to them that haue[3] bene twyfe in parell to beware how they come therin the thyrd tyme.

XXII. *Of the merchaunte that chargyd hys fonne to fynde one to fynge for hys fowle.*

This ftory originates in Joh. de Bromyard, "Summa Prædicantium," Litt. E, viii. § 17 : " Sicut patet de illo qui moriens, vxore executrice facta : bouem pro anima fua legauit vt fertur, vxor vero bouem et gallum fimul ad forum

---

[1] *a thyrd*] Hazl. the thyrd.   [2] *couldeft*] Hazl. coulde.
[3] *haue*] in orig. houe.

ducens: utrumque fimul vendidit hac conuentione: quod emptor pro gallo marcam anglicanam et pro boue obolum daret, quod cum factum fuiffet: obolum pro anima dedit marito." The fame ftory in Ropertus Holkot, "Super Libros Sapientiæ," Reutlingen, 1489, fol. 111. Imitated in Pauli, " Schimpff und Ernft," Strasfburg, 1535, No. 438, fol. 71; in Gerlach, " Eutrapeliarum libri III." Lips. 1656, lib. i. No. 656, p. 157; in J. P. de Memel, "Luftige Gefellfchaft," ed. 1695, No. 622, p. 263; and in " Ein reicher Vorrath Anmuthiger Ergoetzlichkeiten," ed 1702, No. 142, p. 94.

RYCH merchant of london there was which had but one fonne y^t was fomewhat vnthryfty therefore his fader vppon hys deth bed called hym to hym & feyd he knew well y^t he had ben vnthrifty howbeit yf he knew he wold amend hys condiciõs he wolde make hym his executoure & leue hym his goodys fo y^t he wold promyfe[4] to praye for his fowle: & to fynde[5] one dayly to fyng for hym/ whyche thyng to performe hys fon there made a faythfull promyfe. After y^t thys mã made hym hys executoure & dyed/ But after that hys foñe kept fuch ryot y^t in fhort tyme he had wafted & fpend all & had nothynge left but a hen & a cok that was hys faders. It fortunyd than that one of hys

[4] *promyfe*] Hazl. promyfe him.
[5] *& to fynde*] Hazl. and fo fynde.

Frendys came to hym & fayd he was fory y^t he had waftyd fo mych & afkyde hym how he wolde pform hys pmyfe made to hys father y^t he wold kepe one to fing for him.

Thys yong man ãfweryd & fayd by god yet I wyll performe my promyfe/ for I wyll kepe thys fame cok alyue ftyll and he wyll krowe euery daye and fo he fhall fynge euery day for my faders fowle/ & fo I wyll performe my promyfe well ynough.

¶ By thys ye may fe that it is wyfdome for a man to do good[1] dedys hym felf whyle he is here & not to truft to the prayer and promys of hys executours.

XXIII. *Of the mayd wafhyng clothys and anfwered the frere.*

THERE was a mayde ftode by a ryuers fyde in her fmok wafhynge clothys. And as fhe ftoupyd oft tymys in her fmokke[2] cleuyd betwene her butokkes/ By whome there came a frere feynge her and fayde in fport. Mayd mayde take hede for Bayard bytys on the

---

[1] *good*] orig. reads goodys.
[2] *oft tymys in her fmokke*] Hazl. ofttymes, her fmocke.

brydyll. Nay wys mafter frere quod the mayden he doth but wype hys mouth and wenyth ye wyll come & kyffe hym.

¶ By thys ye may fe that a womans[3] anfwer is neuer to feke.

XXIV. *Of the .iii. wyfe men of gotam.*

The fame ftory in "Merie Tales of the Mad Men of Gotam." The firft tale in "Shakefpeare Jeft Books," iii. p. 4.

A CERTAYN man there was dwellynge in a towne callyd Gotam which went to a fayre .iii. myle of[4] to by fhepe/ & as he cam ouer a brydge he met w^t one of hys neybours & told him whether he went/ & he afkyd hym whych way he wold bryng thẽ/ whych fayd he wold brĩg thẽ ouer the fame brydge/ nay quod the other mã but thou fhalt not/ by god quod he but I wyll/ ye other agayn faid he fhuld not/ & he agayn faid he wold bryng them ouer fpyte of his teth & fo fell at wordys/ & at the laft to buffertys that eche one knokkyd other well about the heddys w^t theyre fyftys. To

[3] *a womans*] Hazl. womans.
[4] *iii. myle of*] Hazl. iii. myle for.

whom there cam a thyrd man which was a mylner wyth a ſak of mele vppõ a horſe a neybour of theyrs & partyd them &[1] aſkyd thẽ what was the cauſe of theyr varyaunce/ whych then ſhewyd hym the matter & cauſe as ye haue harde/ Thys thyrd man the mylner thought to rebuke[2] theyr folyſhnes with[3] a famylyer example & toke hys ſak of mele from his hors bak & openyd it & pouryd all the mele in the ſak ouer the bridge into the ronyng riuer wherby all the mele was loſt & ſayd thus. By my trouth neybors becauſe ye ſtryue for dryuyng ouer the brydge thoſe ſhepe which be not yet bought nor wot not wher they be/ me thynkyth therfore there is euyn as mych wyt in your heddys as there is mele[4] in my ſak.

¶ Thys tale ſhewyth you that ſome man takyth vppõ hym to ſhew other men wyſdome when he is but a fole hym ſelf.

[1] *partyd them &*] Hazl. paciently.
[2] *to rebuke*] Hazl. for to rebuke.
[3] *theyr folyſhnes with*] Hazl. them by.
[4] *is mele*] Hazl. is mele now.

MERY TALYS.   47

XXV. *Of the gray frere that anfweryd his penytent.*

A correfponding tale, fee in J. Frey, "Die Gartengefellfchaft," s. 1. & a, cap. 30, fol. 36 verfo: "Von einem Landfknecht, der einem alten Münch beichtet," ed. Frankf. 1590, fol. 29 *verfo*.

MAN there was[5] that came to confeffe hym felf[6] to a gray frere & fhroue him that he had layne with a yong gentilwomã/ yᵉ frere than afkyd hym in what place/ & he faid it was in a goodly chãber all nyght lõg in a fofte warme bed/ The frere heryng that fhruggyd in hys clothys & fayd/ now by fwete feynt fraunces then waft thou verye well at eafe.

XXVI. *Of the gentylman that bare the fege borde on his nek.*

CHANDELER beĩg a wydower dwellĩg at holborne brige in lõdõ had a fayre doughter/ whom a yõg gentylman of dauys Inne woyd gretly[7] to haue hys pleafure of her/ whych by long fute to her made at

---

[5] *there was*] orig. reads there man.
[6] *hym felf*] Hazl. hym.   [7] *gretly*] Hazl. fore.

yᵉ laſt graūtyd him & poyntyd hym to cõe vppõ a night to her faders houſe in yᵉ euenyng & ſhe wold conuey him into her chãber ſecretly whych was an inner chamber wythin her faders chãber/ ſo accordĩg to yᵉ poĩtmẽt all thĩg was pformyd So yᵗ he lay wᵗ her all nyght & made good chere tyll about .iiii.¹ a clok ĩ yᵉ mornĩg/ at which time it fortunyd this yõg gẽtylmã fell a coughĩg/ whych cã vppõ hym ſo ſore yᵗ he coud not refrayn. Thys yong wench² then fering her fader that lay in the next chaūber bad hym go put hys hed in the draught left yᵗ her fader ſhuld here him: which after her councell roſe in hys ſhyrt & ſo dyd/ but thẽ becauſe of the ſauor of the draught it cauſyd hym to cough mich more & louder that yᵉ wẽchis fader hard hym³ & aſkyd of hys doughter what man was that yᵗ coughid⁴ ĩ her chãber/ ſhe anſweryd & ſayd no body. But euer thys yõg mã coughid ſtyll more & more whom the fader heryng ſeyd/ by goddys body here thou lyeſt I wyll ſe who hys there & roſe out of hys bed.

Thys wench perceyuyng⁵ her fader ryſyng cam

¹ *.iiii.*] Hazl. foure.
² *Thys yong wench*] Hazl. Thys wench.
³ *hard hym*] Hazl. herde it.
⁴ *what man was that that coughid*] Hazl. what man it was that coughed.
⁵ *perceyuyng*] Hazl. perceyued.

to the gentylmã & fayd take hede fyr to your felf my fader comyth.⁶ Thys gentylman fodēly therwyth abafhyd wolde haue pullyd hys hed out of the drawght hole whych was very ftreyte for hys hed that he pullyd the fege bord vp therwyth/ & hangyng about hys nek ran vppon the fader beyng an old man & gaue hym a gret fall/ & bare hym down & hurt hys arme/ & openyd the dorys & rã into yᵉ ftrete wyth yᵉ draught borde about hys nek toward dauys Inne as faft as he coud.

This wēch for fere rã out of her faders houfe & cã not there a moneth after. Thys gentylman as he ran vppon holborne brydge met wᵗ a colyers cart laden wᵗ colys where there was .ii. or .iii.⁷ fkyttyfh horfys/ which when they faw thys gentylman rõnyng ftart afyde & threw down yᵉ cart wyth colys/ & drew it afyde & brake yᵉ cart rope/ wherby the colys fell out fome in one place fome in an other/ & after the horfys brake theyr trafys & ran fome toward fmythfeld & fome toward newgate that the colyer rã after them & was ã howre & more or he coud get his horfe to geder agayn/ By whych tyme the people of the ftrete were ryfen and cã to yᵉ ftrete & faw yt ftrawyd wyth colys euery one for hys part gaderyd vp the

⁶ *my fader comyth*] Hazl. for my fader comyth.
⁷ *.ii. or .iii.*] Hazl. two or thre.

colys : that y̆ᵉ moſt part of the colys were gone or the colyer had got hys horſys.

But duryng thys whyle the gẽtylman wẽt thorow ſeynt andrews chyrchyard toward dauys Inne/ & there met wyth the ſextẽ comyng to church¹ to rĩg to morow mas : whych when he ſaw the gentylman in the churchyarde in hys ſhyrt wᵗ the draght bord about hys nek/ had wẽd it had ben a ſpryt : & cryed alas alas a ſpryt & ran bak agayn to hys houſe almoſt at yᵉ barrys & for fere was almoſt out of hys wyt yᵗ he was yᵉ worſe halfe a yere after.

Thys gentlman than becauſe dauys Inne gatys were not open went on the bak ſyde & lept ouer the garden wall/ but in lepyng the ſege bord² ſo trobled hym that³ he fell down in to the garden & had almoſt brokẽ his nek & there ley⁴ ſtyll tyll y the prĩcipall cam in to the gardyn/ whych when he ſaw hym ly there had wend ſom man had be ſlayne & there caſt ouer yᵉ wall & durſt not come nye him tyll he had callyd vp hys company/ whych when many of the gentylmen wher come to gether/ lokyd well vppõ him and knew hym & after releuyd hym/ But the borde

---

¹ *comyng to church*] Hazl. commynge to attend.
² *ſege bord*] Hazl. draught-bord.
³ *that*] in orig. thot.
⁴ *there ley*] Hazl. there he lay.

MERY TALYS.   51

yᵗ was about hys nek cauſyd his hed ſo to ſwell
that they coud not get it of tyll they were fayne⁵
to cutte it of with hatchettys. Thus was the
wench well Japyd/⁶ & for fere ſhe ran frõ her
fader/ her faders arme was hurt the colyar loſt his
colys the ſextẽ was almoſt out of his wyt/ & the
gentylman had almoſt broke his nek.

XXVII. *Of the marchaũtys wyfe that ſeyd ſhe wolde
take a nap at ſermon.*⁷

To take a nap at ſermon or at church is quite a common
ſaying in Germany, ſo common, indeed, that a technical
term "Kirchenſchlaf" has been given to this particular
kind of nap.

MARCHANTYS wyfe ther was in
bowe paryſh in london ſome what
ſtept⁸ in age to whõ her mayd cam
on a ſonday in lent after dyner & ſayd/ mayſtres
quod ſhe they ryng at ſeynt Thomas of acres for
ther ſhall be a ſermõ prechyd anon/ to whom the
mayſtres anſwerd & ſayd mary goddys blyſſyng on
thy hart⁹ for warnyng me therof & becauſe I ſlept

⁵ *fayne*] Hazl. mynded.
⁶ *Japyd*] i. e. mocked.
⁷ *at ſermon*] Hazl. at a ſermon.
⁸ *ſlept*] Hazl. ſlepte.
⁹ *on thy hart*] Hazl. haue thy harte.

not well all this night I pray the brynge my ſtole with me for I wyll go thyder to loke wether I can take a nap there whyle the preſt is prechyng.

¶ By this ye may ſe that many on goth to churche as moche for other thyngys as for deuocyon.

XXVIII. *Of the woman that ſeyd & ſhe lyffyd a nother yere ſhe wolde haue a kokoldis hat of her owne.*

Too imperfect to decipher in Hazl.

THER was a certayn company of women gatheryd to geder in cõmunycacion one happenyd thus to ſay her pyggys after they were farowyd dyed and wolde not lyue and one olde wyfe of her accoyntance heryng her ſay ſo bad her get a cockoldys Hat and put the pyggys therin a whyle after they were farrowyd and they ſholde lyue/ whych wyfe intendyng to do after her counſell came to one of her goſſyppys and ſhewyd her what medecyne was taught[1] her for her pyggys & prayd her to lend her her huſbandys hat/ whych anſweryd her angerly and ſayd I wold

---

[1] *taught*] orig. reads thaugh.

thou knewyſt it Drabbe I haue none for my huſbande is no cookold for I am a good woman and
ſo lyke wyſe euery wyfe anſweryd her in lyke
maner that ſhe departyd frome many of them in
anger and ſkoldynge/ But whan ſhe ſawe ſhe
coude get none ſhe came agayne to her goſſyppys
all angerly and ſayd I haue gone round aboute to
borrow a cookoldys hat and I can get none
wherefore yf I lyue another yere I wyll haue
one of myn own and be out of my neyghbours
daunger.

¶ By this tale a man may lerne that it is more
wyſdome for a man to truſt more to his owne
ſtore than to his neyghbours gentylnes.

xxix. *Of the gentylman that wyſhyd his toth in the gentylwomans tayle.*

A GENTYLMAN & a gentylwoman
ſat togeder talkyn whiche gentylman
had gret payn in one of his teth. &
hapnyd to ſay to the gẽtylwoman[2] thus. I wys
maſtres I haue a toth ĩ my hed which greuyth
me very ſore wherfore I wold yt were in your
tayle. She heryng hym ſaying ſo. anſweryd thus

[2] *gentylwoman*] in orig. gentylwomau.

In good fayth fyr if your toth were in my tale it coud do yt but lytyll good/ but if there be any thynge in my tale that can do your toth good I wold yt were in your toth.

¶ By this ye may fe that a womans anfwer is feldome to feke.

xxx. *Of the welchman that confeſſyd hym how he had ſlayn a frere.*

IN the tyme of lent a welchman cam to be confeſſyd of hys curat whych in hys cõfeſſyon fayd that he had kyllyd a frere/ to whõ the curat fayd he coude not aſſoyle hym/ yet quod the welchmã yf thou kneweſt all thou woldeſt aſſoyle me well enough/ & when the curat cõmandyd hym to ſhew hym all the cafe he fayd thus/ mary ther wer ii freres & I might haue ſlayn them both yf I had lyſt but I let one ſkape therfore maſter curat fet the tone agaynſt the tother & then the offence ys not fo great but ye may aſſoyle me well ynough.

¶ By this ye may fe that dyuers menne haue fo euyll & large cõfcyens that they thynke yf they do one good dede or refrayne from the doynge[1]

---

[1] *from the doynge*] Hazl. from doynge.

of one euyll ſynne that yt ys a ſatysfaccyon[2] for other ſynnis and offencys.

xxxi. *Of the welchman that cowde not get but a lytyll male.*

THERE was a company of gẽtylmen in northãtonſhyre whych went to hunte for deere in the porlews in the gollet beſyde ſtony ſtratford/ Among which gentylmen ther was one which had a walche man to his ſyruaunte a good archer/ whiche when they came to a place where they thought they ſhold haue game/ they made a ſtondyng and poyntyd thys welchman to ſtand by a tre nygh the hye way and bad hym in any wyſe to take hede that he ſhot at no[3] raſkall[4] nor medle nat without it were a male & yf it were a male to ſpare not/ wel quod this welchman let me alone. And whan this walchman had ſtande there a whyle he ſawe moche dere cõmynge/ as well of Auntelere as of Raſcall/ but eur he let them go and toke no hede to theym.

[2] *a ſatyſfaccyon*] Hazl. ſatysfaccyon.
[3] *to take hede that he ſhot at no*] Hazl. to ſhote at no.
[4] *raſkall*] i. e. lean beaſt.

And within an howre after he ſaw come rydyng in the hye way a man of the countrey which had a boget hangynge at hys ſadyll bowe. And whan this walche man had eſpyed hym he bad hym ſtand & began to drawe his bow and bad hym deliuer that lyttyll male that hynge at his ſadell bowe/ Thys man for fere of hys lyfe was glad to delyuer hym his boget/ & ſo dyd & than rode his way & was glad he was ſo eſkapyd. And whan this man of the countrey was gon thys welchman was very glad & went incontynent to ſeke his maſter & at laſt[1] founde[2] hym with his company/ and whã he ſawe hym he come to hym & ſayd thus/ Maſter by cottys plut & her nayle I haue ſtande yonder thys two howrys and I cowd ſe neuer a male but a lytell male that a man had hangyng at his ſadell bow/ & that I haue gotten/ & lo here it is/ and toke his maſter the boget whych he had taken awey from the forſayd man/ for the whyche dede bothe the maſter & the ſeruant were afterwarde in great trouble.

¶ By thys ye may lerne yt ys gret foly for a maſter to put a ſeruant to that beſynes wherof he can nothing ſkyll[3] and wherin he hath nat be vſyd.

[1] *at laſt*] Hazl. at the laſte.   [2] *founde*] in orig. fonude.
[3] *ſkyll*] i. e. know, ſignify.

XXXII. *Of the gentyll woman that fayd to a gentylman ye haue a berde a boue & none benethe.*

 YONGE gentylman of the age of .xx.
yere fome whate dyfpofyd to myrth
and game⁴ on a tyme talkyd with a
gentylwoman⁵ which was ryght wyfe and alfo
mery. this gentyll woman as fhe talkyd with hym
happenyd to loke vppon hys berde/ whiche was
but yong and growen fome what⁶ vppon the
ouer lyppe and but lyttyll growen beneth as all⁷
yonge mennys berdys cōmonly vfe to growe
fayd⁸ to hym thus. Syr ye haue a berde aboue
and none beneth. and he herynge her fay fo/
fayd in fporte/ maftres ye haue a berde benethe
and none aboue/ mary quod fhe/ then fet the tone
agaynft the tother/ which anfwere made the
gentylman fo abafhyd that he had not one worde
to anfwer.

⁴ *game*] Hazl. gaye.
⁵ *gentylwoman*] orig. reads geutylwoman.
⁶ *growen fome what*] Hazl. fomewhat growen.
⁷ *as all*] Hazl. as all other.
⁸ *fayd*] Hazl. and fayd.

XXXIII. *Of the frere that fayd our lord fed .v. M.*[1] *peple with .ij.*[2] *fyſhys.*

THERE was a certayn white frere which was a very glotton and a great nyggyn whyche had an vngracyouſe boy that euer folowyd hym and bare hys cloke/ and what for the frerys[3] glottony & for his chorlyſhnes the boy where he went coude ſkant get mete inough for the frere wolde eet almoſte all hym ſelfe. But on a tyme the frere made a ſermon in the cõtrey wherin he touchyde very many myracles whiche cryſt dyd afore his paſſyon amonge whiche he ſpecyalli reherſyde the myracle that cryſte dyd in fedynge fyue thouſande people wythe fyue louys of brede and with iij lyttell fyſhys and thys frerys boy which caryd not gretely for hys maſter herynge hym ſay ſo and conſyderyng that his maſter was ſo great a churle and glotton anſwered with a loude voyce that all the church hard & ſayd by my trouth mayſter/ Then there were no fryers there. whiche anſwere made all the people to fall on ſuche a lawghynge that for ſhame the frere wente out of the pulpet. and as

---

[1] *v. M.*] Hazl fyue M.   [2] *ij.*] Hazl. iii.
[3] *frerys*] in orig. fterys.

for the frerys boy he than departyd out of the church that the frere neuer faw hym after.

¶ By thys ye may fe that it is honefty for a mã that is at mete to depart with fuche as he has to them that be prefent.

xxxiv. *Of the frankelyne that wold haue had the frere gon.*

A[4] RYCHE fraynklyng dwellyng in the countrey[5] had a freer vfyng to his howfe of whom he coud neuer be ryd & had taryed with him the fpace of a fenyght & neuer depart[6] wherfore the fraynklyng beyng wery of hym/ on a tyme/ as he & his wyfe & this frere fat to geder at fupper faynyd hym felfe very angry with hys wyfe In fomoche he fayd he wolde bete her. This frere pfeyuyng wel what they mẽt fayd thus. mafter franklĩg I haue bene here this feuenyght when ye were frẽdys & I wyll tary here this fortenyght lenger but I wyll fe you frendys agayne or I go.[7] thys man perfeyuyng

[4] A wanting in orig.
[5] *in the countrey*] Hazl. countie.
[6] *& neuer depart*] Hazl. and wold never depart.
[7] *go*] Hazl. depart.

that he coude no good nor wolde not depart by none honeſt meanys anſweryd hī ſhortly & ſayd by god freere but thou ſhalte abyde here no lenger & toke hym by the ſhulders & thruſt hym out of the dorys by vyolence.¹

¶ By this ye may ſe that he that wyll lerne no good by example/ nor good maner² to hym ſhewyd is worthy to be taught with open rebukes.

xxxv. *Of the good man that ſayd to his wyfe he had yll³ fare.*

A parallel ſtory is found in the " Complete London Jeſter," ed. 1771, p. 73.

FRER Lymytour⁴ come into a pore mannys howſe in the countrey and becauſe this pore man thought this frere myght do hym ſome good he therfore thought to make hym good chere/ But becawſe hys wyfe wolde dreſſe hym no good mete for coſte/ he therfor at dyner tyme ſayde thus/ By god wyfe

---

¹ *by vyolence*] Hazl. of the houſe.
² *nor good maner*] Hazl. in a maner.
³ *yll*] Hazl. euyll.
⁴ *Lymytour*] i. e. begging-friar.

bycawfe thou dyddeft dreffe me no good mete to my dyner/ were it nat for mafter frere/ thou fholdeft haue half a dofyn ftrypes. Nay fir quod the frere I pray you fpare nat for me/ wherwith the wyf was angry & therfore at foupper fhe caufed them to fare wors.

¶ By thys ye may fe it is good polycy for geftys yf they wyll haue any good chere to pleas alway the wyfe of the howfe.⁵

xxxvi. *Of the frere that bad hys chylde make a laten.*

Too imperfect to decipher in Hazl.
For an analogous account of the refults of inftruction in Latin, fee Bonaventure des Periers, " Les Contes ou les Nouvelles Récréations," &c. Nouv. Ed. par De la Monnaye, tom. i. Nouv. 23, Amfterd. 1735, p. 233 : " Du jeune fils qui fit valoir le beau Latin que fon Curé lui avoit monftré."

HERE was a frere whiche though he were well lernyd yet he was callyd wycked of condycyons whiche had a Gentylmannys fonne to wayte vpon hym and to teche hym to fpeke latyn.

⁵ The moral is wanting in Hazl.

Thys frere came to thys chyldes fader dwellyng in he contrey/ and becawſe this frere wold haue this Gentylman to knowe that this chylde had metly well ſpent[1] his tyme for the whyle he had bene with hym/ he bad this chyld to make in latyn ſhortly Freres walke in the cloyſter. This chylde halfe aſtonyed bycawſe his maſter bad hym make this latyn ſo ſhortly anſwered at all aduentures and ſayd In circuitu impii ambulant.

xxxvii. *Of the gentylman that aſkyd the frere for his beuer.*

IN the terme tyme a good old gentylman beyng a lawyer cam to london to the terme & as he came he hapened to ouertake a frere which was ſom vnthryft & wẽt alone without his beuer wherfor this gẽtylman aſked this frere where was his beuer that ſhold kepe hym cõpany and ſayd it was[2] contrary to his relygyon to go alone/ and it wolde cawſe people to ſuppoſe hym to be ſom apoſtata or ſome vnthryft. By god ſyr quod the frere my felow cõmendeth hym vnto your maſterſhyp/ why[3]

---

[1] *ſpent*] orig. reads ſpeut.   [2] *was*] in orig. waa.
[3] *why*] in orig. who.

quod the gentylman I knowe hym nat/ than quod the frere to the gentylman ye are the more to blame[4] to aſke for hym.

¶ By this tale ye may ſe that he that geueth coũſel to an vnthryft[5] and techeth hym his dutye ſhall haue oftentymes but a mocke for his labour.

XXXVIII. *Of the .iii.[6] men that chaſe the womã.*

The allotment of the two parts of a woman occurs in an old German poem, " Die Theilung." See Von der Hagen, " Geſammtabenteuer," vol. i. Stuttg. & Tübing. 1850, No. 18 :—

" 1475. Hêre wie habt ir iuch bedâht?
   iſt iuwer wille volbrâht,
   Welch teil ir nemen welt?"
   mit züchten antwurt' ir dir helt:
  " ſo wil ich, vrouw', an dirre ſtunt
1480 iu die rede tuon kunt,
   Und will es lenger niht verdagen,
   ich wil es ûf genâde ſagen:
   Das oberſte teil ſol weſen mîn." &c.

Alſo in Don Juan Manuel, " El Conde Lucanor," No. 41, where the vice (el mal) leaves the upper half of a ſervant girl to the virtue (el bien) and keeps the lower part for

  [4] *to blame*] Hazl. fole.
  [5] *an vnthryft*] Hazl. any vnthryft.
  [6] *iii.*] Hazl. thre.

herself. Imitated in one of G. E. Lessing's poetical tales, "Die Theilung;" see Schriften, Berlin, 1838, vol. i. p. 210; also in "Lyrum Carum," 256.

THRE gentylmē cam into an Inne where a fayre woman was tapster wherfor as these thre sat ther makyng mery echone[1] of thē kyssed her & made good pastyme & plesure. howbeit one spake meryly & sayd I can not se how this gentylwoman is able to make pastyme & pleasure to vs all thre excepte that she were departed in thre partes. By my trouthe quod one of theym/ yf that she myght be so departed[2] than I wolde chose for my parte her hed and her fayre face that I myght alway kysse her. Then quod the secōd I wold haue the brest and hart for ther lyeth her loue. Then quod the thyrd then ther is nothyng lefte for me but the loynys buttokkys & leggys & I[3] am content to haue yt for my part. And when these gētylmen had passyd the tyme ther by the space of one hour or ij they toke ther leue & were goynge away but or they[4] went the thyrd man that had chosen the bely & the buttokkys dyd kys the

---

[1] *echone*] Hazl. eche.
[2] *be so departed*] Hazl. be departed.
[3] *& I*] Hazl. I.
[4] *they*] orig. reads thye.

tapyſter & bad her farewel. what quod the furſt mã that had choſen the face & the mouth why doſt thou ſo/ thou doſt me wronge to kys my parte that I haue choſen of her. O quod the other I pray the be not angry for I wolbe[5] cõtent that thou ſhalt kys my part for it.

xxxix. *Of the gẽtylmã that taught his cooke the medeſyne for the tothake.*

IN Eſſex there dwellyd a mery gentylman which had a cooke callyd Thomas that was gretly dyſeaſyd with the toth ake & complainyd to his mayſter there of whiche ſayd he had a boke of medycĩs & ſayd he wold loke vp his boke to ſe whether he cowd fynde any medecyn ther[6] for it & ſo ſende one of hys doughters to his ſtudy for his boke and incontynent lokyd vppon yt a longe ſeaſon & than ſayde thus to hys coke. Thomas quod he here is a medeſyne for thy[7] tothake & yt ys a charme but it wyll do you no good except ye knele on your knee[8] and aſke yt for ſeynt charyte. Thys

[5] *I wolbe*] Hazl. I am.
[7] *thy*] Hazl. your.
[6] *ther*] Hazl. therin.
[8] *knee*] Hazl. knees.

man glad to be releaſyd of hys payne knelyd & ſayd mayſter for ſeīt charyte let me haue that medecyne. Then quod thys gentylman knele on your knees & ſay after me which knelyd doūe and ſayd after hym as he bad hym.

Thys gētylman began & ſayd thus. The ſone on the ſonday. The ſone on the ſonday quod thomas. The mone on the monday. The mone on the monday. the trynyte on the tewſday. the trinyte on the tewſday. The wite õ the wednyſ-day the wit on the wednyſday. The holy holy thurſday. The holy holy thurſday. And all that faſt on fryday. and al that faſt on fryday. Shite in thy mouthe on ſaterday. This Thomas coke herynge his mayſter thus mokkynge hym in an anger[1] ſtart vp & ſayd/ by goddys body mok-kyng churle I wyll neuer do the ſeruyce more. And wente forth to hys chāber to get hys gere to geder to thentent to gon thens by & by. But what for the anger that he toke with hys maſter for the moke that he gaue hym & what for labour that he toke to geder hys gere ſo ſhortly to geder the payne of the tothake wente from hym incontynent that his maſter com to hym & made hym tary ſtyll[2] & tolde hym that hys charme

---

[1] *in an anger*] Hazl. in anger.
[2] *tary ſtyll*] Hazl. to tarry ſtyll.

was the cauſe of the eaſe of the payn of his tothake.³

¶ By this tale ye may ſe that anger oftymys puttyth away bodely payne.⁴

XL. *Of the gētylmā that promyſyd the ſcoler of Oxford a ſarcenet typet.*

Similar tales in Legrand d'Auſſy, fabliaux: " Les trois Aveugles de Compiègne," tom. iii. p. 1; Pellbartus, " Pomerium quadrageſimale," Aug. Vind. 1502, fol. i. ſermo 38 c. Benecke, " Beitraege zur Kenntniſs der altdeutſchen Sprache und Literatur, Bd. 2, Gottingen, 1832: " Der Pfaffe Amis," V. 2043-2472; Sozzini, Nov. 1; Franco Sacchetti, No. 140; Giov. Franc. Straparola, "XIII. Piacevoli Notti," No. 13, fav. 2. Alſo in " Nouveaux Contes à rire," Cologne, 1702: " Le Rotiſſeur Filouté," p. 261; and in " Scoggin's Jeſts," 1626: " How Scogin deceived the Draper," repr. 1864, p. 137.

SCOLER of Oxford lately made maſter of arte come to the cyte⁵ of lōdon & in polys met with the ſayd mery gētylmā of eſſex which was euer dyſpoſyd to playe many

³ *his tothake*] Hazl. the tothake.
⁴ *bodely payne*] Hazl. the bodely payne.
⁵ *come to the cyte*] Hazl. cam in to the cyte.

mery paieantys with whome before he had bene of famylier accoyntance and prayd hym to geue hym a fercenet typet. This gentylman more lyberall of promys than of gyft grantyd hym he fholde haue one yf he wolde come to his lodgynge to the figne of the bulle without byfhops gate in the next mornynge at vi of the cloke. Thys fcoler thanked hym & for that nyght departed to hys lodgynge in flete ftrete/ & in the mornynge erely as he poynted cam to hym to the fygne of the bull/ Anon as[1] this gentylman faw hym he bad hym go with hym in to the Cite & he fholde be fped anone/ which incontynent went togeder tyll they[2] cam in to feynt laurence churche[3] in the Jury wher the gentylman efpyed a preft rauefhyd to maffe & tolde the fcoler that yonder is the prefte that hathe the typet for you & bade hym knele down in the pewe & he wolde[4] fpeke to hym for it/ And incontynent this gentilman went to the preft and fayd Syr here is a fcoler and kynf-man of myne greatly dyfeafed with the chyn-cowgh.[5] I pray yow when maffe ys done gyue hym iij draughtys of your chales. The preft

---

[1] *Anon as*] Hazl. And as.
[2] *they*] in orig. fhe; Hazl. he.
[3] *churche*] in orig. churhe.
[4] *wolde*] Hazl. fhold.
[5] *chyncowgh*] i. e. hooping-cough.

graūted hym & turned hym to the ſcoler and
ſayd Syr I ſhall ſerue you as ſon as I haue ſayd
maſſe. the ſcoler thē taryed ſtyl & hard the maſſe
truſtīg then whan[6] the maſſe was done that the
preſte wolde geue hym his typet of ſarcenet. Thys
gentylman in the meane whyle departed out of
the churche. This preſt whan maſſe was don
put wyne in the chalice & cam to the ſcoler
knelyng in the pew profferyng hym to drink of
the chales. this ſcoler lokyd vpon hym & muſed
& ſayd/ maſter perſon[7] wherfore profer ye me
the chalyce mary quod the preſte for the gentylman tolde me ye were dyſeſyd with the chīcough
& prayd me therfore that for a medcyn ye myght
drynk of the chalis. Nay by ſeynt mary quod
the ſkolar he promyſyd me ye ſholdd delyuer me
a typet of ſercenet. Nay ſayde the preſte he ſpake
to me of no typet/ but he deſyryd me to gyue
you drynk of the chales for the chyncough. By
goddys body quod the ſcoler he is as he was euer
wont to be but a mockyng wrech/ & euer I lyue
I ſhall quyte it hym & ſo departyd out of the
churche ī gret āger.

¶ By thys tale ye may perceyue it were no
wyſdom for a man to truſt to a man to do a

---

[6] *then whan*] Hazl. that whan.
[7] *maſter perſon*] Hazl. why, maſter parſon.

thynge that ys contrary to hys olde accuſtumyd condycyons.

XLI. *Of maſter ſkelton that brought the byſhop of Norwich .ii. feſantys.*

The ſame ſtory, with very little alteration, in " Certain Merrie Tales of Skelton, Poet Laureat," 1567. See Skelton's Works, ed. A. Dyce, London, 1843, p. liii; compare " Scoggin's Jeſts : " " How Scogin was new chriſtened, and confirmed a Knave by the French biſhop," repr. 1864, p. 130.

IT fortuned ther was a gret varyaūce betwen the byſshop of Norwhich & one mayſter Skelton a poyet lauriat. In ſo moch that the byſshope cōmaunded hym that he ſholde nat come in at hys gatys.[1] This maſter ſkelton dyd abſent hym ſelfe for a longe ſeaſon but at the laſt he thought to do his duty to hym and ſtudyed wayes how he myght obtayn the byſhopys fauour and determynyd him ſelfe that he wold com to hĩ with ſome preſent & humble hym ſelfe to the byſhop & gat a couple of feſants and cam to the byſhoppys place & requyryd the porter he myght come in to ſpeke wyth my lorde.

[1] *in at hys gatys*] Hal. in his gatys.

this porter knowyng hys lordys pleaſure wolde
not ſuffer hym to come in at the gatys/ wherfore
this maſter ſkelton went on the bak ſyde to ſeke
ſome other way to com in to the place. But
the place was motid that he cowd ſe no waye to
come ouer except in one place where there lay a
longe tre ouer the motte in maner of a brydg that
was fallyn downe with wynd wherfore this maſter
ſkelton went a long vppon the tre to com ouer &
when he was almoſt ouer hys fote ſlyppid for
lake of ſure fotyng & fell in to the motte vp to the
myddyl but at the laſt he recoueryd hym ſelfe
& aſwel as he coud dryed hym ſelfe agayn/ &
ſodenly cam to the byſhop beyng in his hall then
lately ryſen from dyner which when he ſaw ſkelton
cõmĩg ſodẽly ſayd to hym why thow chatyfe I
warnyd the thow ſholdys neuer come yn at my
gatys & chargyd my porter to kepe the owt.

Forſoth my lorde quod ſkelton though ye gaue
ſuche charge & though your gatys be neuer ſo
ſuerly kept/ yet it is no more poſſyble to kepe
me owt of your dorys than to kepe out crowes
or pyes for I cãe not in at your gatys. but I
came ouer the motte that I haue bene almoſt
drownyd for my labour & ſhewd hys clothys
how euyll he was arayed which cauſyd many
that ſtode thereby to laugh a pace. Then quod
ſkelton yf it lyke your lordeſhyp I haue brought

yow a dyſshe to your ſupper a cople of Feſantys. Nay quod the byſhop I defy the and thy Feſantys alſo And wreche as thou art pyke the out of my howſe for I wyll none of thy gyft. How be it with as humble wordys as he coud this ſkelton deſyryd the byſhop to be hys good lorde & to take his lytyll gyft of hym/ But the byſhop callyd hym dawe¹ & fole often tymys & in no wyſe wolde receyue that gyft. This Skelton than conſyderyng that the byſhop callyd hym fole ſo oft ſayd to one of his famyliers therby that though it were euyl to be criſtynyd a fole yet it was moche worſe to be confyrmyd a fole of ſuche a byſhop for the name of confyrmacyõ muſt nedes abyde/ therfore he ymagynyd how he might auoyd that cõfyrmaciõ & muſyd a whyl & at the laſt ſayd to the byſhop thus. if your lordſhyp knew the namys of theſe feſãtys ye wold be cõtẽt to take them/ why caytyf quod the byſhop haſtely & angerly what be theyre namys. I wys my lorde quod ſkelton this Feſant is callyd alpha. ys. primus² the furſt. & this is callyd O that ys nouiſſimus the laſt. & for the more playn vnderſtandyng of my mīde. If it pleſe your lordſhyp to take them I pmyſe you This Alpha is the fyrſt that euer I gaue you & this O is the laſt that euer I wyl

---

¹ *dawe*] i. e. fool.
² *ys. primus*] Hazl. which is in primys.

gyue you wyl I leue. at the which³ ãſwer al that wer by made gret laghter & al they deſyryd the byſhop to be good lord to hĩ for hys mery conceytys at whoſe⁴ requeſt or they went the byſhop was cõtent to take hym vnto his fauour⁵ agayn.

¶ By thys ye my ſe that mery conceytes dothe a man moche more good than to frete hym ſelfe with anger and melancoly.

XLII *Of the yeman of gard that ſayd he wold bete the carter.*

A YOMAN of the kynges gard dwellyng in a vyllage beſyde london had a very fayre yonge wyfe. To whom a cart of the towne a tal felowe reſorted & lay with her dyuers tymes whan her huſband was from home/⁶ & ſo⁷ openly knowẽ that all the town ſpake therof/ wherfor ther was a yong man of the towne well accoynted with this yemã of gard that tolde hym

    ³ *the which*] Hazl. which.
    ⁴ *whoſe*] Hazl. which.
    ⁵ *fauour*] orig. reads fauonr.
    ⁶ *was from home*] Hazl. was on garde.
    ⁷ *& ſo*] Hazl. and this was ſo.

that fuche a carter had layne by his wyfe. To whome thys yeman of garde fayd & fware by godys body that yf¹ he met hym² it fhold coft hym his lyfe. Mary quod the yong man yf ye go ftreyght euyn now the hye way ye fhall ouertak hym dryuĩg of a cart³ ladyn with hay toward london wherfore this yeman of garde⁴ incontynent rode after this carter/ & within fhort fpace ouertoke hym & knew hym well ynough/ & incõtynent called the cart to hym & fayd thus. Sirra I vnderftand that thou doft ly euery night with my wyfe when I am from home. This carter beyng no thyng afrayd of the other/⁵ anfwered ye mary what than/ what than quod the yeman of garde/ by goddes hart haddeft thou na tolde me the trouth⁶ I wolde haue broken thy hede. And fo the yeman of garde retourned and no hurte done nor ftroke ftryken nor profered.

¶ By thys ye may fe that the greateft crakers fomtyme whan it cõmeth to the profe⁷ be mofte cowardys.

    ¹ *that yf*] Hazl. if.
    ² *met hym*] Hazl. mette with hym.
    ³ *of a cart*] Hazl. a cart.
    ⁴ *of garde*] Hazl. of the garde.
    ⁵ *of the other*] Hazl. of him.
    ⁶ *trouth*] Hazl. truth.
    ⁷ *profe*] orig. reads profe.

XLIII. *Of the pryſt that ſayd our lady was not ſo curyous a woman.*

N the towne of Bottelley dwelled a mylner whiche had a good homely wench to his doughter whom a curat⁸ of the next towne louyd/ and as the fame went had her at his pleſure.

But on a tyme this curat preched of theſe curyous wyues now a dayes/ & whether it were for the nones⁹ or whether it come out at all aduenturys he hapned¹⁰ to ſay thus in his ſermõ. Ye wyues ye be ſo curious in all your warkes that ye wote nat what ye mene/ but ye ſhold folowe our lady. For our lady was nothynge ſo curyous as ye be/ but ſhe was a good homely wenche lyke the mylners doughter of bottellay. At which ſayng all the paryſhons made gret laughynge/ & ſpecyally they that knewe that he had loued¹¹ the ſame¹² wenche.

¶ By thys ye may ſe it is great foly for a man that is ſuſpected with any parſon to prayſe or

---

⁸ *a curat*] Hazl. the curate.
⁹ *for the nones*] i.e. for the purpoſe.
¹⁰ *hapned*] Hazl. had penyd.
¹¹ *he had loued*] Hazl. he louyd.
¹² *the ſame*] Hazl. that ſame.

to name the fame parfon openly left it bryng hym forther in fclaunder.

XLIV. *Of the fole that wold go to the deuyll.*[1]

This tale is taken from Joh. de Bromyard, "Summa Prædicantium," Litt. P, xii. § 39 : " De quodam domino, qui fatuum fuum infirmum frequenter cum per illum tranfiret, confortari folebat. dicendo : Spera in deo : ibis ad cœlum. Cui ille femper refpondit : nolo illuc ire : a quo cum uno dié quereret : quare nollet illuc ire. Refpondit : quia volo ire ad infernum, quare inquit : quia inquit. diligo te : & ficut fui tecum in vita, ita volo tecum effe in morte. & poft mortem : & quia tu ibis ad infernum : ita volo ego ratione focietatis. Cui dominus. quomodo fcis. quod ego illud vadam : quia inquit. tota patria loquitur fic. dicentes. quod tu es peffimus homo. et ideo ibis ad infernum : Et in veritate : qui malus homo fuit prius. ex verbis illius compunctus : optime fe poftea correxit." Repeated in Pauli, " Schimpff und Ernft," Strafb. 1535, No. 43 : " Von einem Narren der nit zu Gott faren wolt."

FOLE there was that dwellyd with a gētylmā ī the contray whiche was callyd a great tyraunt and an ectorcyoner. But this fole louyd his mafter merueloufly becaufe he cheryfyd hym fo well. It

---

[1] Hazl. Of the fole that faide he had leuer go to hell than to heuen.

happenyd vppon a feafone one of the gentylmans feruauntys fayde to the fole. as they talkyd of fermon matters/ by my trowth Jak quod he wolde to god that thou and I were both of vs in heuyn. Nay by lady quod the fole I wyll not go to heuyn for I had leuer go to hell/ than the other afkyd hym why he had leuer go to hell. By my trouth quod the fole for I wyll go with my mafter & I am fure my mafter fhall go to hell/ For euery man feyth he fhall go the deuyll in hell therefore I wyll go thyther with hym.

XLV. *Of the plowmannys fonne that fayd he faw one make² a Gofe to kreke fweetly.*

THERE was a certayn ploughmannys fonne of the contrey of the age ofe .xvi. yeres that neuer come moche among company but alwey wēt to plough and hufbandry/ on a tyme this yong lad wēt to a weddynge with hys fader where he fee one lute vppon a lute. And when he came home agayne³ at nyght his moder afkyd hym what fport he hade at weddynge. This lad anfweryd and fayd by my trouth moder

² *make*] Hazl. to make.   ³ *home agayne*] Hazl. home.

quod he ther was one that brought in a gofe betwene hys armys[1] and tykled her fo vppõ the nek that fhe crekyd the fwetlyeft that euer I hard gofe creke in my lyfe.

XLVI. *Of the maydys anfwere that was with chylde.*

N[2] a marchauntys houfe in london there was a mayd whiche was gotten[3] with chylde to whome the maftres of the houfe came & chargyd[4] her to tell her who was the fader of the chylde. To whome the mayden anfweryd forfoth no body / why quod the mayftres yt ys not poffyble but fome mañe mufte be[5] the fader thereof. To whome the mayd fayd /[6] why maftres why may not I[7] haue a chylde without a man afwell as a hen to lay[8] eggys wythout a cok.

¶ Here ye may fe it is harde to fynde a woman wythout an excufe.

[1] *brought in a gofe betwene hys armys*] Hazl. brought a gofe in his armes.
[2] *In*] Hazl. At.   [3] *gotten*] Hazl. great.
[4] *& chargyd*] Hazl. and that commanded.
[5] *mufte be*] Hazl. is.   [6] *fayd*] Hazl. anfwered.
[7] *not I*] Hazl. I not.
[8] *a hen to lay*] Hazl. hennys lay.

XLVII. *Of the feruant that rymyd with hys mafter.*

In John Pet. de Memel, ed. 1695, No. 62, the fame ftory occurs; the German verfes are the more draftic, as the fervant's anfwer has no rhyme:—

        Ich heiffe Sylvefter
        Und fchlaf bei deiner Schwefter.
Der knecht antwortete:
        Junker ich heifs Hans,
        Und fchlaf bei Eurer Frau.

GENTYLMAN there was dwellynge nygh kyngfton vppon Temys. rydynge[9] in the contrey wyth hys feruaunte which was not the moft quyckyft felow But rode alway fadly by hys mayfter and hade very few wordys. Hys mayfter fayde to hym Johñ quod he why rydyft fo fadly[10] I wold haue the tell me fom mery talys to paffe[11] the tyme with. by my trouth mafter quod he I can tell no talys/ why quod the mafter[12] cãft[13] not fyng. no by my trouth quod hys feruaunt[14] I cõwd neuer fyng in

[9] *rydynge*] Hazl. and rydynge.
[10] *fo fadly*] Hazl. thou fo fadly.
[11] *paffe*] Hazl. beguyle.
[12] *why quod the mafter*] Hazl. Then fayd his mayfter.
[13] *canft*] Hazl. canft thou.
[14] *quod his feruaunt*] Hazl. quod he.

all my lyfe/ why quod the mafter¹ canft thou ryme than/² By my trouth mafter³ quod he I can not tell but yf ye wyll begynne to ryme I wyll folow as well as I can. by my trouthe quod the mafter that is well fayd⁴ than⁵ I wyll begyn to make a ryme let me fe howe well thou canft folowe/ fo the mafter mufyd a whyle⁶ and than began to ryme thus. Many mennys fwannes fwymmys in temmys and fo do myne.

Then quod the feruaunt. And manny men lye⁷ by other mennys wyues and fo do I by thyne/ what doft horfon⁸ quod the mafter/ by my trouth mafter nothynge quod he but make vp the ryme. but quod the mafter I charge the tell me why thou fayft fo/ forfothe mafter quod he for nothynge in the worlde but to make vp your ryme. Then quod the mafter yf thou do it⁹ for nothyng ellys

---

¹ *why quod the mafter*] Hazl. quod the mayfter.

² *ryme than*] Hazl. ryme.

³ *By my trouth mafter . . . I cannot tell*] Hazl. No by my trouthe . . . I can not.

⁴ *well fayd*] Hazl. well.

⁵ *fayd than*] Hazl. therfore.

⁶ *fo the mafter mufyd a whyle*] Hazl. thy mafter meanewhyle.

⁷ *And manny men lye*] Hazl. And many a man lyeth.

⁸ *horfon*] Hazl. thou, horefon.

⁹ *do it*] Hazl. doift.

I am content,[10] So the mafter forgaue hym his faynge all though he had fayd trewth.[11]

XLVIII. *Of the welchman that delyueryd the letter to the ape.*

The origin of this tale is again Joh. de Bromyard, " Summa prædicantium," Litt. J. vii . § 6 : " Quidam aulam cuiusdam nobilis intrans : videnfque fymiam de fecta filiorum veftitum : quia dorfum ad eum habebat : filium credidit effe domini : cui cum reverentia qua debuit loqueretur : inuenit effe fymiam fuper eum chachinantem : cui ille malediceris inquit : credidi quod fuiffes iankyn filius domini mei." Reprinted in Th. Wright, " Latin Stories," &c. Lond. 1842, No. 129, " Filius domini." Imitated in " Jack of Dover," 1604 ; " The foole of Hampſhire ;" " Percy Society," vol. iii. p. 30. It. in " Lyrum Carum," 141.

A KNYGHTE in Myddylfex had a feruaunt which had commytted a felony wherof he was endyted/ and becaufe the terme drew nye he fered he fholde be fhortly arayned therof & in ieoperdye of his lyfe. wherfor in all the hafte fent a letter by a walchmã a feruaunt of hys vnto the kynges Juftyce of the

---

[10] *content*] orig. reads concent.
[11] *he had fayd trewth*] Hazl. he fayd trouthe peraduenture.

kynges bench requyrynge hym to owe his lawfull fauour to hys feruant and cōmaunded hys feruant fhortly to brynge hym an anfwere/ This walche man came to the chefe Juftyce place and at the gate fawe an ape fyttynge there in a cote made for hym as they vfe to apparel apys for dyfport/ This walchman dyd of hys cap & made curtefy to the ape and fayd my mafter recōmendeth hym to my lorde your fader & fendeth hym here a letter. Thys ape toke thys letter and opened it and loked theron/ and after loked vpon the man makyng many mockes and mowes as the properte of apys is to do/ this welchman becawfe he vnderftode hym nat came agayn to his mafter accordyng to his cōmaundement and fayde he had delyuered the letter vnto my Lorde chefe Juftyces fonne whiche fat at the gate in a furred cote/ Anone his mafter afked hym what anfwere he had whiche fayd he gaue hym an anfwere but it was outher Frenche or Latyn for he vnderftode hym nat/ but fyr quod he ye nede nat to fear for I fawe by his countenance fo moche that I warant you he wyll do your errand furely[1] to my lorde hys fader. Thys gentylman in truft[2] therof made none other labour. For lacke wherof hys feruant that had done the felony

---

[1] *your errand furely*] Hazl. your errand.
[2] *truft*] orig. reads trnft.

within two dayes³ after was rayned at the kynges benche & caſt and afterwarde hangyd.

¶ By this ye may ſe that euery wyſe man ought to take hede that he ſende no folyſshe ſeruant vpon a haſty meſſage that is a mater of weyght.

XLIX. *Of hym that ſold ryght nought.*

Such difficult taſks or enigmatical queſtions are of very frequent occurrence in the literature of the middle ages. Generally known is the one taken from Juſtini, " Hiſtor. Philipp." lib. 18, cap. 3; repeated in " El libro de los enxemplos," No. 347; reprinted in " Bibl. de Aut. Eſpañ." tom. 51, Madr. 1860, and in Joh. Gallenſis, " Summa collectionum," pars ii. diſt. 1, cap. 4. s. l. 1493, fol. In another, firſt mentioned by Ratherius, (d. 974) " Sermo 3 de octavis paſchae," d'Achery, " Spicilegium," ed. 1723, fol. i. 395, (ſee Haupt, "Zeitſchrift f. deutſches Alterthum," vol. viii. p. 21), a man has to come to his prince half riding, half walking, and to bring with him his friend and his enemy; he comes with his right foot in the ſtirrup, walking with the left, and brings with him his dog as his beſt friend and his wife (whom he makes denounce him as a murderer) as his worſt enemy. This is repeated, with many alterations, in the " Geſta Romanorum," cap. 124; " Altdeutſche Blätter," ed. by Haupt and Hoffmann, Leipzig, 1836, vol. i. pp. 149, 154; " Scala celi," 50; Pauli, " Schimpff und Ernſt,"

---

³ *two dayes*] Hazl. a month.

1535, No. 400, fol. 75; Hans Sachs, Nürnberg, 1591, fol. vol. ii. p. 4, fol. 59, "Der Hecker mit den drei feltzamen ſtücken;" Die Schildbürger, cap. 21, in von der Hagen, Narrenbuch, Halle, 1811, p. 129; Ferd. Wolf, "Ueber die neueſten Leiſtungen der Franzoſen für die Heraufgabe ihrer National-Heldengedichte," Wien, 1833, p. 135; Cf. Würdtwein, "Dioceſis Moguntina in Archidiaconatus diſtincta," Mannhemii, 1749, tom. i. p. 488, and Loiſeleur Deſlongchamps, "Fables Indiennes," tom. ii. p. 125; "Cento Novelle Antiche," nov. 100, Torino, 1802, p. 183; and together with many ſimilar jokes in "Salomon and Markolph" (in von der Hagen, Narrenbuch, p. 236, ſeq.) Finally, Grimm's "Kindermaerchen," Goettingen, 1856, No. 94 (cf. vol. iii. p. 170) contain a ſimilar tale, "Die kluge Bauerntochter;" a girl has to come to the king not clothed, not naked; not riding, not driving; not in the way, not out of the way. She wraps a large fiſhing-net round her and comes dragged in the rut by a rope tied to the tail of an aſs.

A CERTAYNE felow there was which proffered a dagger to ſell to a felowe of his whiche anſwered hym and ſayde that he had right nought to geue hym therfor. wherfor the other ſayd that he ſhold haue his dagger vpon condycyon that he ſhoulde geue and delyuer vnto hym therfore within vi. dayes after right nought/ or els xl. ſhilynges in money/ wherto this other was content. Thys bargayn thus agreyd he that ſholde delyuer thys ryght nought toke no thought vntyll ſuche tyme that the day apoynted drewe nye. At the whiche tyme he began¹ to Immagyne how he myght gyue hym² right nought. And fyrſt of all he thought on a feder/ a ſtrawe/ a pynnes poynte/ and ſuche other. But no thynge coud he deuyſe but that it was ſomwhat/ wherfor he come home al ſad & penſyfe for ſorow of leſynge of xl. ſhyllynges/ & coud nouther ſlepe nor take reſt/ wherof his wyfe beynge agreuyd demaūded the cawſe of his heuynes/ whiche at the laſt after many denayes tolde her all, well ſyr quod ſhe let me herewith alone & gete ye furthe a towne/ and I ſhall handle this³ well ynough. This man folowynge his wyues councell went forthe of the towne & let his wyfe ſhyft.

This woman than henge vp an yerthen pot wherof the botom was out vpon the wall by a corde. And whan thys other man come and aſked for the good man ſhe ſayd that he was nat within/ But Syr quod ſhe I know your erand wel ynough/ For I wote well ye wold haue of myn huſbonde xl. ſhyllynges becauſe he can nat delyuer to you this day right nought/ Therfore ſyr quod ſhe put your hande into yonder potte and take your money/ this man beyng glad thruſt

¹ *he began*] in orig. be began.
² *hym*] Hazl. this man.
³ *this*] Hazl. this matter.

his[1] hand in[2] suppoſyng to haue taken xl. ſhyllynges of money & thruſt his hand vp thrugh[3] vp to the elbow/ quod the wyfe than Syr what haue ye there. Mary quod he Ryght nought. Syr quod ſhe than haue ye your bargeyn & than my huſbond hath contentyd you for his dagger accordynge to his promyſe.

¶ By this ye may ſe that often tymes a womans wyt at an extremyte is moche better than a mannys.

L. *Of the frere that told the iii.[4] chylders fortunys.*

In Joh. Pet. de Memel, "Luſtige Geſellſchaft," 1695, No. 253, p. 110, a friend gives the following reply to the queſtion of a father about the employment his three ſons ſhould undertake: "If the one was a beggar, the other a thief and the third a murderer, they would all be well off for life," meaning thereby the ſame profeſſions the friar recommends in our tale. It. in Moncaut, "Contes populaires," 50; "Luſtigmacher," 2, 50.

THERE was a certayn limytour which went a limytīge to a certeyn vyllage wherin dwelled a certayn ryche man of whome he neuer cowde gette the valew of an

[1] *his*] orig. reads hir.   [2] *in*] Hazl. in it.
[3] *vp thrugh*] Hazl. thoroughe it.   [4] *.iii.*] Hazl. thre.

halfpeny/ yet he thought he wolde go thyder agayn to aſſay⁵ them. And as he went thyderward the wyfe ſtondynge at the dore perceyuynge him cõmynge a farre of thought that he wolde come thyder and by & by ran in & bad her chyldren ſtandyng at the dore that yf the frere aſked for her ſay ſhe was nat within. The frere ſaw her ron in and ſuſpected the cawſe and come to the dore and aſked for the wyfe/ the ſhyldren as they were byddyn/ ſayde that ſhe was not within/ than ſtode he ſtyl lokyng on the chyldren/ and at the laſt he called to hym the eldeſt & bad hym let hym ſe his hande/ and whan he had ſene his hande O Jheſu quod he what fortune for the is ordeyned/ Than called he the ſeconde ſonne to ſe his hande/ and his hande ſene the frere ſayde/ O lord what a deſteny is for the⁶ preparyd. Than loked he in the thyrd ſoñes hand/ ſuerly quod he thy deſtenys is hardeſt of all/ & therwith wente he his way. The wyfe herynge theſe thynges ſodenly ran out and called the frere agayne/ and firſt made hym to come in/ and after to ſyt downe and ſet before hym the beſt mete that ſhe had/ and whan he had well etyn & dronken ſhe beſought hym to tell her the deſtenyes of her chyldren/ which at the laſt after

⁵ *to aſſay*] Hazl. and aſſaye.
⁶ *is for the*] Hazl. for the is.

many denayes tolde her that the fyrſt ſholde be a beggar. The ſecond a thefe. The third an homycyd/ whiche ſhe heryng fell downe in a ſowne & toke it greuouſly. The frere conforted her and ſayd/ that though theſe were theyr fortune yet there myghte be remedy had. Than ſhe beſought hym of his counſell. Than ſayd the frere ye muſt make the eldeſt that ſhalbe a begger a frere. and the ſecond that ſhalbe a thefe a man of law/ & the third that ſhalbe an homycyde/ a phiſycyon.

¶ By this[1] ye may lerne that they that wyll come to the ſpeche or Preſence of any parſon for theyr owne cawſe they muſt fyrſt endeuer theyme ſelfe to ſhewe ſuche maters as thoſe parſons moſte delyte in.

LI. *Of the boy that bare the frere hys maſters money.*

A CERTAYN frere had a boy that euer was wont to bere this freres money and on a tyme whan the boy was farre behynde his maſter as they two walked togeder by the way there met a man the frere whiche knewe that the boy bare the frerys money and ſayde. How Mayſter frere/ ſhall I byd thy boy

---

[1] *this*] Hazl. this tale.

MERY TALYS.   89

hye hym apace after the/ Ye quod the Frere Than went yᵉ man to yᵉ boy & fayd fyre thy mayfter byddyth yᵉ gyueth me xl. ꝺ.² I wyll not quod the boy then called the man with a hye voyce to yᵉ frere & fayd fyr he fayth he wyll not/ then quod the frere bete hym/ & when the boy herde his mayfter fay fo he gaue the man .xl. pens.

¶ By this ye may fe it is foly for a man to fay ye or nay to a matter except he knowe fuerly what the matter is.

LII. *Of Phylyp fpencer the bochers man.*

(Gerlach), " Eutrapeliarum," lib. ii. No. 58, p. 16, relates a very fimilar ftory; the butcher's name is David, and his fervant cries out to the friar, " You can have no more meat until you pay your bill." The fame in " Roger Bontems en belle Humeur," Cologne, 1731, tom. i. p. 119, " Naïveté d'un Valet:" " Point d'Argent point de Tripes:" and in " Nouveaux Contes à rire et Aventures plaifantes de ce Temps," 3ᵉ édit. Cologne, 1702, p. 102: " Sans Argent point de Tripes."

A CERTAYN bocher dwellyng in faynt Nicholas flefhamels in london callyd Poule had a feruaũt callyd Peter. This Peter on a fonday was at yᵉ chirche heryng

² *.xl. d.*] Hazl. xl pens.

maſſe & one of his felawes whoſe name was Phylip ſpencer was ſent to call hym at the comaundement of his mayſter. So it happened at the tyme that the curat prechyd. And in his ſermon touched many auctorytees of the holy ſcrypture. Amonge all the wordes of the pyſtell of ſaynt Poule ad philippenſes/ that we be[1] not onely bound to beleue in cryſt but alſo to ſuffer for cryſtys ſake & ſayd theſe wordes in ye pulpet/ what ſayth Poule ad philippenſes to this. This yõge man y^t was called Philip ſpencher had went he had ſpoken of hym anſwered ſhortely & ſayd/ mary ſyr he bad Peter come home & take his parte of a podyng for he ſholde go for a calfe anone. The curat heryng this was abaſhyd & all the audyence made grete laughter.

¶ By this tale[2] ye may lerne[3] that it is no token of a wyſe man to gyue a ſodayne anſwere to a queſtiõ before that[4] he knowe ſuerly what the matter is.

[1] *that we be*] Hazl. howe be.
[2] *this tale*] Hazl. this.
[3] *lerne*] Hazl. ſe.
[4] *before that*] Hazl. before.

LIII. *Of the courtear and the carter.*

A correſponding tale in "Scoggin's Jeſts:" "How Scogin told thoſe that mocked him, that hee had a wall-eye." Reprint. 1864, p. 106.

THER came a courtyer by a carter the whiche in deryſyon preyſed the carters bak legges and other members of his body meruelouſly whoſe geſtyng the carter perceyued & ſayd he had another property than ye courtyer eſpyed in hym/ & whan the courtyer had demaūded what it ſholde be/ he loked aſyde ouer his ſholder vpon the courtyer & ſayd thus/ lo ſyr this is my properte.

I haue a wall eye in my hed/ for I neuer loke ouer my ſholder this wyſe but I lyghtly eſpye a knaue.

¶ By this tale a man maye ſe that he that vſed to deryde and mocke other folkys/ is ſomtyme hym ſelfe more deryded & mocked.

LIV. *Of the yonge man that prayd his felow to tech hym his pater noſter.*

In the "Nouveaux Contes à rire," &c. Cologne, 1702, p. 248, " D'un Homme à qui on apprit à prier à Dieu," a corresponding tale occurs; the priest uses a very effective means of teaching the Pater noster to a niggard pawnbroker: he bids him lend money to all the people he should send him. So he first sends a man called "Pater noster," living at a place called "Qui es in cœlis," then another of the name of "Sanctificetur," coming from "Nomen tuum," &c.

YONG mã of yᵉ age of .xx. yere rude & vnlernyd in yᵉ tyme of lẽt cã to his curat to be cõfessyd¹ whiche whẽ he was of his lyfe serched & examyned coude not say his Pater noster/ wherfore his cõfessour exorted hym to lerne his Pater noster/ & shewed hym what an holy & goodly prayer it was/ & the effect therof/ & the vii petycyons therin cõteyned. The fyrst petycyõ begynneth. Pater noster. &c. yᵗ is to saye. O fader halowyd be thy name amõge mẽ in erth as amõge aũgels in heuen. The ii. Adueniat. &c. Let thy kyngdome come & regne thou amonge vs men in erth as amonge aũgels in heuen. The .iii. Fiat. &c. Make vs to fulfyl thy wyll here in erth as thy aũgels in heuen. The .iiii. Panẽ nostrũ. &c. Gyue vs our dayly sustenaũce alwaye & helpe vs as we gyue & helpe² them yᵗ haue nede of vs. The .v. Dimitte. &c. Forgyue vs our synnes

---

¹ *confessyd*] orig. reads tofessyd.
² *gyue & helpe*] Hazl. haue and helpe.

done to the as we forgyue them yt trefpas agaynfte vs. The .vi. Et ne nos. Let vs not be ouercome with euyll temptacyõ. The .vii. Sed libera. &c. But delyuer vs frõ all euyll amen.

And then his confeffour after this expofycyõ to hym made inioyned hym in penaũce to faft euery fryday brede & water³ tyll he had his Pater nofter well & fuffycyẽtly lerned. This yonge man mekely acceptyng his penaunce fo departed & came home to one of his cõpanyons & fayd to his felow. fo it is that my goftly fader hath gyuen me in penaũce to faft euery fryday brede & water tyll I can fay my Pater nofter/ therfore I pray ye teche me my Pater nofter/ & by my trouth I fhall therfore teche the a fonge of Robyn hode that fhall be worth .xx. of it.

¶ By this tale ye maye lerne to knowe the effect of the holy prayer of the Pater nofter.

LV. *Of the frere that prechyd in ryme expownyng the aue maria.*

The latter portion of this tale is repeated in "Scoggin's Jefts," 1626, Mr. Hazlitt's reprint, p. 76.

³ *brede & water*] Hazl. on brede and water.

A CERTAYN frere there was whiche upō our lady day the Annūcyacyon made a fermon in the whyte frerys in London/ and began his anteteme¹ this wyſe/ Aue maria gracia plena dominus tecũ/ &c.

Theſe wordes quod the frere were ſpoken by the aungel Gabryel to our lady when ſhe cõceyued Cryſt/ whiche is as moche to ſay in our moder tõgue as all heyle Mary well thou be yᵉ ſone of god is wᵗ the. And further more the aūgell ſayd/ thou ſhalte conceyue and bere a ſone. And thou ſhalt call his name Jeſum/ and Elyzabeth thy ſwete coſyn/ ſhe ſhall conceyue the ſwete ſaynt Johñ. And ſo procedyd ſtyll in his Sermon in ſuche fond ryme that dyuers & many gentylmen of the court that were there begã to ſmyle & laugh. The frere yᵗ perceyuynge ſayd thus Mayſters I pray you harke I ſhall tel you a narraciõ.

There was ones a yong preeſt yᵗ was not all the beſt clark ſayd maſſe & rede a coleɕt thus Deus qui viginti filij tui &c. Where² he ſholde haue ſayd vnigeniti filij tui. &c.

And after whẽ mas was done there was ſuche a gentylmã as one of you are³ now yᵗ had herde

---

¹ *anteteme*] Hazl. antetexte.   ² *Where*] Hazl. wherfore.
³ *are*] orig. reads at.

his maſſe came to ye preeſt & ſayd thus. Syr I pray you tell me how many ſonnys had god almyghty/ quod ye preeſt why aſke you y^t. Mary ſyr quod ye gentylman I ſuppoſe he had .xx. ſonnys/ for ye ſayd ryght now. Deus qui viginti filii tui. The preeſt perceyuyng how y^t he derydyd hym anſwerde hym ſhortly & ſayd thus. How many ſonnys ſo euer god almyghty had/ I am ſure y^t thou art none of them for thou ſkornyſt ye worde of god. And ſoo ſayd the frere in the pulpet. No more ar ye none of ye chylderẽ of god. For ye ſkorne & laugh/ at me now y^t preche to you the worde of god. which wordys made the gentylmen and all the other people laughe moche more thã they dyd before.

¶ By this tale a man may lerne to perceyue well y^t the beſt the wyſyſt & ye moſt holyeſt matter y^t is by found pronunciatyon & vtterauce may be marryd/ nor ſhall not[4] edyfye to ye audyẽce. Therfore euery proces wolde be vtteryd with wordys & cõtenaũce cõuenyent to the matter.

Alſo yet by this tale they that be vnlernyd in ye latyn tongue maye knowe the ſentence[5] of the aue maria.

[4] *nor ſhall not*] orig. reads nor ſhall nor.
[5] *ſentence*] Hazl. ſeſtence.

LVI. *Of the curat that prechyd the artycles of the Crede.*

The "Miracle-play" alluded to in this ſtory is not contained in the collection of pageants known under the name of "Ludus Coventriæ," (publiſhed by the Shakeſpeare Society: "Ludus Coventriæ; a Collection of Myſteries," edited by J. O. Halliwell, London, 1841), and repreſented at Coventry on the Feaſt of Corpus Chriſti, as the twelve Articles of the Creed are not mentioned in any of them. According to Collier, "The Hiſtory of the Engliſh Dramatic Poetry," vol. ii. Lond. 1831, p. 138, the MS. preſerved in the Britiſh Muſeum ("Bibl. Cotton. Veſpas." D. viii.)' was written at leaſt as early as the reign of Henry VII, and therefore it may well be that at the time the "Hundred Mery Talys" were compiled, or, at any rate, the preſent tale was written, another ſeries of "Myſteries" was performed at Coventry on that occaſion. This ſuppoſition is confirmed by a notice from the "MS. Annals, Codex Hales," quoted by Th. Sharp in his "Diſſertation on the Pageants or Dramatic Myſteries anciently performed at Coventry," Coventry, 1825, 4to. p. 11: "1519-20. New Plays at Corpus Chriſti Tyde which were greatly commended."

There is, however, another collection of "Myſteries," the "Cheſter Plays, formerly repreſented by the trades of Cheſter at Whitſuntide," (edited as one of the publications of the Shakeſpeare Society, by Th. Wright, vol. i. Lond. 1843; vol. ii. Lond. 1847,) which has in the play No. 22, "The Emiſſion of the Holy Ghoſt," (vol. ii. p. 134,) the very verſes alluded to in the preſent tale. As this work is not in everybody's hands I think myſelf juſtified in quoting the verſes in full:

"*Petrus.*

I beleeve in God omnipotente,
That made heaven and eirth and firmament,
With steadfaste harte and trewe intente,
And he is my comforte.

Andreas.

And I beleeve more I be lente,
In Jesu his sonne from heavensente,
Vereye Christe that us hath kente,
And is our elders lore.

Jacobus Major.

And I beleeve, with boste,
In Jesu Christe, in mightest moste,
Conseveith through the holye ghoste,
And borne was of Marye.

Johannes.

And I beleeve, as I cane see,
That under Pilate suffred he,
Skourged and nayled on roode tree,
And buryed was his fayer bodye.

Thomas.

And I beleeve, and south can tell,
That he ghostlye wente to helle:
Delivered his that their did dwell,
And rose the thirde daie.

Jacobus Minor.

And I beleeve fully this,
That he steyed up to heaven blesse,
And on his fathers righte hande is,
To raigne for ever and aye.

Philippus.
And I beleeve, with harte fteadfafte,
That he will come at the lafte,
And deeme mankinde as he has cafte,
Bouth the quicke and the dead.

Barthelemewe.
And my beleffe fhalbe mofte
In vertue of the holye ghofte,
And through his helpe, without bofte,
My life I thinke to leade.

Mathieus.
And I beleeve, through Godes grace,
Suche beleffe as holye church has,
That Godes bodye graunted us was
To ufe in forme of bredde.

Symon.
And I beleve with devocion
Of fynne to have remiffion,
Through Chriftes bloode and paffion,
And heaven, when I am dead.

Jude.
And I beleeve, as all we mon,
In the generall refurrexcion
Of eiche bodye, when Chrifte is borne
To deme bouth good and evill.

Matheus.
And I beleeve, as all we maye,
Everlaftinge life after my daye
In heaven to have ever and aye,
And fo overcome the devill."

In a third collection, the "Towneley Mysteries," which might possibly have contained corresponding verses, "The Emission of the Holy Ghost" is lost by a lacuna in the MS.

IN a vyllage in warwyck shere there was a paryshe preest & thoughe he were no gret clark nor graduat of ye vnyuersyte/ yet he prechyd to his paryshons vpõ a sonday/ declaryng to thẽ y^e .xii. artycles[1] of the Crede. shewynge them that the fyrst artycle was to beleue in god the fader almyghty maker of heuen & erth. The second. To beleue in Jesu Cryste his onely sone our lorde coequall with ye fader in all thynges perteynyng to ye deyte. The thyrd that he was cõceyuyd of the holy goost Borne of the vyrgyn Mary. The fourth that he suffred deth vnder ponce pylate/ & that he was crucyfyed dede & beryed. The fyft that he descendyd to hel & fet[2] out ye good sowlys y^t were in fayth & hope/ & that he[3] ye thyrd day rose from deth to lyfe. The syxth he assendyd in to heuen to ye ryht syde of god ye fader wher he syttyth. The seuenth y^t he shall come at the day of dome to Judge both vs that be qvik &

---

[1] *the .xii. artycles*] Hazl. xii. artycles.
[2] *fet*] i. e. fetched.
[3] *and that he*] Hazl. and than.

them that be dede. The eyght to beleue in the holy gooſt equall god wᵗ the fader & the ſone. The nynth in holy chyrche¹ Catholyke & in the holy comunyõ of ſayntys. The tenth In yᵉ remyſſyon of ſynnes. The leuynth In the reſurreccyõ generall of yᵉ body and ſoule. The twelfth In euerlaſtynge lyfe that god ſhall reward thẽ that be good. And ſayd to his paryſhons further yᵗ theſe artycles ye be bounde to beleue for they be trew &² of auctoryte. And yf you beleue not me/ thẽ for a more ſuerte & ſuffycyẽt auctoryte/ go your way to couentre/ and there ye ſhall³ ſe them all playd in corpus criſti playe.

¶ By redyng of this tale they yᵗ vnderſtõde no latyn may lerne to knowe the .xii. articles of the fayth.

LVII. *Of the frere that prechyd the .x. comaundementys.*

The diviſion of the Decalogue followed in this tale is taken from Exodus xx; it was adopted by the Council of Trent and uſed by the whole Latin Church. Luther approved of it, and it is ſtill in uſe with the entire Lutheran denomination. The diviſion now employed by the Church of England is the ſame which has always been uſed by the

---

¹ *holy chyrche*] Hazl. the holy churche.
² *trew &*] Hazl. trewe.
³ *ſhall*] orig. reads ye ye ſhall.

Greek Church. It was ſtrongly recommended by Calvin in 1536, adopted by Bucer and the Tetrapolitans, and is to be found in any Engliſh formulary ſince 1537. Mr. Hazlitt's conjecture for the lacuna in his edition, p. 82, is therefore inadmiſſible; and this is more clearly ſhown by the fact, that in his interpolation either the ſeventh or eighth commandment is omitted. To judge from the undamaged paſſages, however, there muſt have been ſome difference between Mr. Hazlitt's original and mine: the text of the mutilated copy cannot have read but thus: *The eighth, not to bear falſe witneſs againſt thy neighbour.* THE NINTH AND TENTH, *not to couete nor deſyre no mannes goodes vnlefully. Thou ſhalt not deſyre thy neyghbours wyfe*, &c., this being exactly the form, which was nearly excluſively uſed ſince its acceptation by the Council of Trent Catechiſm. It is likewiſe found in Maſkell's and Biſhop Hilſey's Primers.

The ſeven deadly ſins have always been the ſame, but their diviſion is ſometimes different. See Mr. Hazlitt's edition, p. 83, note 2, and Maſkell's "Prymer," in "Monum. Ritual. Eccles. Anglic." vol. ii. p. 178, London, 1846.

LIMITOUR of the gray frerys in London whiche prechyd in a certayn vyllage in the countrey in the tyme of his lymitacyõ/ & had but one ſermõ[4] which he had lerned by hart y^t was[5] of ye declaryng of the .x. cõmaũdemētes. The fyrſt to beleue in one god/ & to honour hym aboue all thynge. The

---

[4] *& had but one ſermon*] Hazl. and had prechyd a ſermon.   [5] *that was*] Hazl. that.

secõd to swere not in vayn by hym nor none other[1] of his creatures. The thyrde to abstayne from worldly operacyõ on ye holy day thou & all thy seruantys of whõ thou hast charge. The fourthe to honor thy parẽtys & helpe thẽ in theyr necessyte. The fyfth to sle no man in dede nor wyll nor for no hatred[2] hurte his body nor good name. The syxt to do no fornycacyõ actuall/ nor by no vnlefull thought to desyre no fleshly delectacyõ. The seuenth to stele nor depryue no mãnes goodes by thefte robbery extorcyõ/ vsery/ nor dysceyt. The eyght to bere no false wytnesse to hurt another/ nor to tell no lyes/ nor to say nothyng agaynst trewthe. The nynth to couet nor desyre no mañys goodes vnlefull. The tenth to couet nor to desyre[3] thy neyghbours wyfe for thyn owne appetyte vnlefully.

And becauſe this frere had preched this sermon so oftyn/ one y^t had hard it before told the frerys seruaũt y^t his mayster was callyd frere Johñ .x. cõmaũdementes wherfor this seruaũt shewed ye frere his mayster therof/ and aduysed hym to preche some sermon of some other matter/ for it greuyd hym to here his mayster so deryded/ & to

---

[1] *none other*] Hazl. none.

[2] *hatred*] Hazl. orig. reads hated.

[3] *The tenth to couet nor to desyre*] Hazl. thou shalt not desyre.

be called frere Johñ .x. cõmaũdemẽtys/ for euery man knoweth what ye wyll fay as foone as euer ye begyn bycaufe ye haue preched it fo oft.

Why than quod yᵉ frere I am fure thou knoweft well which be yᵉ .x. cõmaũdementys yᵗ haft harde thẽ fo oft declaryd/ ye fyr quod the feruaũt yᵗ I do. Then quod the frere I praye the reherfe thẽ vnto me now. Mary quod yᵉ feruaũt thefe be they.[4] Pryde Couetyfe Slouth Enuy wrath Glotony and Lechery.

¶ By redynge this tale ye maye lerne to knowe the .x. cõmaundementes and the .vii. dedely fynnes.

LVIII. *Of the wyfe that bad her hufband ete the candell furft.*

This tale is imitated by John Cotgrave, " Wits Interpreter, the Englifh Parnaffus," 1662, p. 282.

THE hufbande fayde to his wyfe thus/ wyfe[5] by this candell I dremed this nyght that I was a cokolde.[6] To whome fhe anfwered and fayd hufbonde. By

[4] *thefe be they*] Hazl. they be thefe.
[5] *to hys wyfe thus/ wyfe*, &c.] Hazl. to his wyfe thus wyfe, &c.   [6] *a cokolde*] Hazl. cocke colde.

this brede ye are none. Thẽ fayd he/ wyfe ete the brede. She anfwerd & fayd to her hufbande/ then ete you the candell for you fware fyrſt.

¶ By this a man may fe that a womans anfwere is neuer to feke.

LIX. *Of the man of lawys fonnys anfwer.*

A WOMAN demaũdyd a queſtyon of a yong[1] chyld fonne vnto a mã of lawe of what craft his fader was/ which chyld fayd his fader was a crafty man of lawe.

¶ By this tale a man may perceyue that fome-tyme peraduenture yõge Innocentys fpeke truely vnduyfed.

LX. *Of the frere in the pulpit that bad the woman leue her babelyng.*

N a certayn paryſh chyrche in London after the olde lawdable & accuſtomyd maner there was a frere mynor all though he were not the beſt clark nor coude not

---

[1] *yong*] Hazl. little.

make the beſt ſermon/ yet by the lycence of the curat he there preched to the paryſhons.² Among the whiche audyence there was a wyfe at that tyme lytyll dyſpoſyd to contemplacyõ talkyd with a goſyp of hers of other feminyne tales/ ſo loud that the frere hard & ſomwhat was perturbyd therwith. To whom therfore openly the frere ſpake & ſayd. Thou woman there in the tawny gow/³ hold thy peace & leue thy babelyng thou troblyſt the worde of god.

This woman there with ſodeynly abaſhyd bycauſe yᵉ frere ſpake to her ſo openly yᵗ al yᵉ people her beheld anſweryd ſhortly & ſayd/ I beſhrewe hye hard⁴ that babelyd more of vs two. At yᵉ whyche ſeyng yᵉ people dyd laugh bycauſe they felt but lytyll fruyte in his ſermon.

¶ By this tale a man may lerne to be ware how he openly rebukyth any other & in what audyence leſt it tourne⁵ to his owne reprofe.

² *paryſhons*] orig. reads paryſhous.
³ *gow*] Hazl. gowne.
⁴ *hye hard*] Hazl. his harte.
⁵ *tourne*] Hazl. come.

LXI. *Of the welchman that caſt the ſkot in to the ſee.*

IN the rayne of the moſt myghty and vyctoryous Prynce kynge Henry the viii. cruell warre began betwene Englyſshe men Frenſhemen/ & Skottys. The Englyſshemen were ſo myghty vpon yᵉ ſe that none other people of other realmys were able to reſyſt thẽ/ wherfore they toke many grete enterpryſys/ & many ſhyppys/ & many pryſoners of other remys yᵗ were theyr enmys. Among the which they happenyd on a ſeaſon to take a ſkottys ſhyp. & dyuers ſkottys they ſlew & toke pryſoners. Among whom ther was a welchmã that had one of the ſkottys pryſoner & bad hym that he ſhold do of his harnes/ which to do the Skot was very loth/ howbeyt for fere at yᵉ laſt he pullyd it of wᵗ an yuyll wyll/ & ſayde to yᵉ welchmã/ yf thou wilt nedys haue my harnes take it there/ & caſt it ouer the bord in to the ſe. The welchman ſeyng that ſayd. By Cottes blut & her nayll. I ſhall make her fat¹ it agayn. And toke hym by yᵉ legges & caſt hym after ouer the bord in to the ſe.

¶ By this tale a man maye lerne yᵗ he that is

¹ *fat*] i.e. fetch.

subget to another ought to forsake his owne wyll/ & folow his wyll & cōmaūdement yt so hath subieccyon ouer hym/ lest it torne to his gretter² hurt & damage.

LXII. *Of the man that had³ the dome wyfe.*

The same story in the " Scolehouse of Women," 1542. Reprinted in (Utterson's) " Select Pieces of Early Popular Poetry," vol. ii. p. 73-74, Lond. 1825.

THERE was a man that maryed a woman whiche hath grete ryches & bewte/ how be it she had suche an impedyment of nature that she was dome and coude not speke/ whiche thynge made hym full ofte to be⁴ ryght pēsyfye & sad/ wherfore vpon a daye as he walkyd alone ryght heuy in hart thynkīg vpō his wyfe. Ther came one to hym & askyd hym what was the cause of his heuynes/ which answeryd that it⁵ was onely bycause his wyfe was borne dome. To whō this other sayd. I shall shewe ye soone a remedy & a medycyn therfore that is thus. Go take an aspen lefe & lay it vnder her tōgue this nyght she beyng a slepe/ & I warrant the yt

---

² *gretter*] Hazl. great. ³ *had*] orig. reads bad.
⁴ *full ofte to be*] Hazl. to be. ⁵ *it*] in orig. is.

ſhe ſhall ſpeke on the morow/ whiche man beyng glad of this medycyne preparyd therfore/ & gatheryd aſpen leues. Wherfore he layd .iii.[1] of them vnder her tõge whẽ ſhe was a ſlepe. And vpon ye morowe whẽ he hym ſelf wakyd he deſyrous to know how his medycyne wroughte beyng in bed w^t her demaunded[2] of her how ſhe dyd/ & ſodenly ſhe anſweryd & ſayd. I beſhrewe your hart for wakynge me ſo erly/ & ſo by vertew of y^t medycyne ſhe was reſtored to her ſpeche.

But in cõcluſyon her ſpeche ſo increſyd day by day & ſhe was ſo curſt of cõdycyõ that euery day ſhe braulyd & chyde[3] with her huſbande ſo moche y^t at ye laſt he was more vexyd and had moche more troble & dyſſeaſe with her ſhrewed wordes then he had before whan ſhe was dome.

Wherfore as he walked another tyme alone he happened to mete agayne with the ſame perſon that taught hym the ſayde medycyne. And ſayde to hym this wyfe.

Syr ye taught me a medycyne but late to make my dome wyfe to ſpeke. Byddyng me laye an aſpen lefe vnder her tonge when ſhe ſlepte. And I layd .iii. aſpen leues there. wherfor now ſhe

---

[1] *.iii.*] Hazl. thre.
[2] *demaunded*] Hazl. he demaunded.
[3] *chyde*] i. e. made an inceſſant noiſe.
[4] *alone*] Hazl. abrode.

speketh. But yet she speketh so moche and so shrewdly that I am more wery of her now than I was before when she was dome.

Wherfore I praye you teche me a medycyne to modyfye her that she speke not so moche.

This other answeryd and sayd thus. Syr I am a deuyll of hell. But I am one of them that haue leeft power there. Albeyt yet I haue power to make a woman to speke. But yet yf[5] a woman begyn ones to speke/ I nor all the dyuels in helle that haue the moft[6] power be not able to make a woman to be ftyll/ nor to caufe her to leue her spekynge.

¶ By this tale ye may note that a man oftymes defyreth and coueteth to moche[7] that thynge that oft torneth to his dysplefure.

LXIII. *Of the proctor of arches that had the lytell wyfe.*

This tale may be taken from Ottomarus Luscinius, "Joci ac Sales mire Festivi," s. l. 1524, 8vo. No. 50, sign. D 3, *verso:* "Mulier parva minus malum," where it is told of Aristoteles; it was appropriated by Joh. Gastius, "Convivalium Sermonum," lib. i. p. 313, Basil, 1549:

[5] *But yet yf*] Hazl. but and if.
[6] *the moft*] Hazl. the more.
[7] *to moche*] Hazl. moche.

"De uxore parva," and alſo by E. Walgemuth, "500 Friſche und verguldete Haupt-Pillen," s. l. 1669, ii. No. 30, p. 56. In the "Nouveaux Contes à rire," &c. Cologne, 1702, it is told of Leonidas of Lacedemon, and is likewiſe contained in the "Complete London Jeſtes," 1771, p. 65; Certayne Conceyts, 14; Conceits, 81; repr. in Shakeſp. "Jeſt Books," iii. pp. 8, 24. Item, Lyrum Carum, 87; Schreger, 17, 114, p. 567.

ONE aſkyd a proctoure of Arches lately before maryed why he chaſe hym ſo lytell a wyfe/ whiche anſwerede becauſe he had a text ſaynge thus. Ex duobus malis minus malum[1] eſt eliendum/ that is to ſaye in englyſshe. Amonge euyll thynges the leſt is to be choſen.

LXIV. *Of the .ii.[2] nonnys that were ſhryuyn of one preſt.*

IN the tyme of lente there cam two nonnys to ſaynt Johns in london by-cauſe of the greate pardon there to be confeſſyd. Of yᵉ whiche nonnys the one was a yonge lady & the other was olde. This yonge lady choſe fyrſt her Confeſſoure/ and confeſſyd her that ſhe had ſynned in Lechery. The con-

---

[1] *minus malum*] Hazl. minus malis.
[2] *the .ii.*] Hazl. ii.

feſſoure aſked w^t whom it was. She ſayde it was with a luſty Gallāt. He demaūdyd where it was. She ſayd in a pleaſaunt grene herber. He aſkyd further whẽ it was. She ſayd in ye mery moneth of May. Then ſayd ye confeſſour this wyfe. A fayre yong lady/ with a luſty gallant/ in a pleaſaunt herber/ in ye mery³ moneth of May/ ye dyd but your kynde. Now by my trouth god forgyue you & I do.

And ſo ſhe departed and incõtynent the olde nõne met with her aſkynge her how ſhe lyked her confeſſour/ whiche ſayde that he was⁴ the beſt goſtly fader y^t euer ſhe hadde And the moſt eaſyſt in penaunce geuynge.

For cõfort wherof this other nonne went to the ſame confeſſour. And ſhroue her lykewyſe that ſhe had ſynned in Lechery. And he demaunded with whom/ which ſayde with an olde Frere/ he aſkyd where. She ſayd in her olde cloyſter. He aſkyd what ſeaſon. She ſayd in lent. Then the confeſſour ſayd thus.

An olde hore to lye with an olde frere/ in the olde cloyſter/ in the holy tyme⁵ of Lent. By cokkys body yf god forgyue the yet wyll I neuer forgyue the.

    ³ *in the mery*] Hazl. and in the mery.
    ⁴ *that he was*] Hazl. he was.
    ⁵ *in the holy tyme*] Hazl. and in the holy tyme.

Whiche wordys caufyd her to departe all fad and fore abasfhyd.

¶ By this tale men may lerne that a vycyoufe acte is more abhomynable in one perfon than in an other/ in one feafon than in an other and in one place than in an other.

LXV. *Of the efquyer that fholde haue bene made knyght.*

WHEN the moft noble and fortunate prynce Edwarde of Englonde made warre in Fraunce with greatte puyffaunce and Armye of People. Whome the Frenche kynge with a nother grete hoft incounteryd. And when bothe ye hoftis fhulde Joyne & the trumpettis began to blow/ a yong fquyer of englonde rydyng on a lufty courfer of whiche horfe the noyfe of ye trūpettys fo prykkyd ye courage y^t the fquyer coude not hym retayne/ fo that agaynft his wyll he ran vpon his enemys whiche fquyer feynge none other remedy fet his fpere in the reft/ and rode trough the thykkyft of his enemys/ & in conclufyon had good fortune and fauyd hymfelfe alyue without hurt/ & the englyfh hoft folowyd & had the vyctory. And after when ye felde was done[1] this kyng Edwarde called the ſquyer/ & bad hym knele downe for he wolde make hym knyght/ becauſe y[t][2] he valyauntly was yᵉ man[3] yᵗ day which with the moſt couragyouſe ſtomak aduenturyd fyrſt vpon theyr enemys. To whom yᵉ ſquyre thus anſwerde. Yf it lyke your grace to make any body knyght therfore/ I beſeche you to make my horſe knyght & not me/ for certes it was his dede & not myne/ & full ſore agaynſt my will.

Whiche anſwere the kynge herynge refraynyd to promote hym to the order of knyghthode/ reputynge hym in maner but a cowarde/[4] & euer after fauoryd hym the leſſe.[5]

¶ By this tale a man may lerne how it is wyſdome for one that is in good credence to kepe hym therin/ and in nowyſe to dyſable hymſelfe to moche.

[1] *done*] Hazl. wonne.
[2] *becauſe that*] Hazl. becauſe.
[3] *man*] orig. reads men.
[4] *but a cowarde*] Hazl. but for a cowarde.
[5] *the leſſe*] Hazl. the leſſe therfore.

LXVI. *Of the man that wold haue the pot stand there as he wold.*[1]

The same story is related in the "Scole-house of Women," 1542; vide "Select Pieces of Early Popular Poetry," Lond. 1825, vol. ii. p. 77-78, "*All though the mete therin were not inough, sodenly cõmaundyd her.*" Mr. Hazlitt considers this passage very corrupt: but the use of the word "*ynough*" in No. 92 shows, plainly enough, that his supposition is false.

A YONGE man late maryed to a wyfe thowght it was good polycy to get the mayftry of her in the begynnynge. Cam to her the pot sethynge ouer yᵉ fyre all though the mete therin were not inough sodenly cõmaundyd her to take the pot from the fyre. whyche answeryd & sayde that yᵉ mete was not redy to ete. And he sayd agayne I wyll haue it taken of for my pleasure. This good woman loth yet to offend hym set yᵉ pot besyde the fyre as he bad.[2] And anone after he cõmaũded her to set the pot behynde the dore/ & she sayd therto agayne ye be not wyse therin. But he precisely sayd it sholde be so as he bad. And she gentylly

---

[1] Hazl. Of hym that wolde gette the maystrye of his wyfe.   [2] *bad*] in orig. had.

agayne did his cōmaūdement. This man yet not fatysfyed cōmaunded her to fet the pot a hygh vpon the hen roft/ what quod yᵉ wyf agayne³ I trow ye be mad. And he fyerfly than cōmaunded her to fet it there or els he fayd fhe fholde repēt⁴ She fomewhat aferde to moue⁵ his pacience toke a ladder and fet it to the rooft/ and wēt herfelf vp the ladder and toke the pot in her hande prayeng her hufbande than to holde the ladder faft for flydynge/ whiche fo dyd.

And whenne the hufbande lokyd vp and fawe the Potte ftande there on hyght⁶ he fayde thus. Lo now ftandyth the pot there as I wolde haue it This wyfe herynge that fodenly pouryd the hote potage on his hed & fayd thus. And now bene the potage there as I wolde haue them.

¶ By this tale men may fe it is no wyfedome for a man to attempte a meke womās pacyēce to far left it torne to his owne hurte & damage.

³ *what quod the wyf agayne*] Hazl. What! quod the wyfe.
⁴ *repent*] Hazl. repent it.
⁵ *moue*] in orig. mone.
⁶ *on hyght*] orig. reads an hyght.

LXVII. *Of the penytent that fayd the fhepe of god haue mercy vpon me.*

In G. Wickram, "Der Rollwagen," Frankf. 1590, fol. 47, *verfo*: "Von einem einfaeltigen Bawren der da beichtet vnd kundt nicht beten," this ftory has been amplified: until St. John's Day the penitent fays, "the lamb of God have mercy upon me;" afterwards, "the fheep of God;" and later in the year, about the beginning of autumn, "the wether of God." In Kirchhof, "Wendunmuth," Frankf. 1573, i. fol. 255, *verfo*: "Ein Schaefer lehrnet betten," he fays, "the wether of God," after the prieft has reproved him for faying "the fheep of God." Item in Nafr-eddin's "Schwänke," 1857; No. 105. p. 43; cf. No. 115, p. 47.

CERTAYNE confeffour in the holy tyme of lente inioyned his penitent to fay dayly for his penaunce this prayer. Agnus dei miferere mei/ whiche was as moche to faye in englyfshe as yᵉ Lambe of god haue mercy vpon me. This penitens acceptynge his penaũce departyd & that tyme twelfe moneth after came agayne to be confeffyd of the fame cõfeffoure whiche demaundyd of hym whether he had fulfyllyd his penaũce that he hym inioynyd yᵉ laft yere. And he fayd thus/ ye fyr I thank god I haue fulfylled it/ for I haue fayde thus to daye mornynge¹ and fo dayly. The fhepe of

---

¹ *mornynge*] Hazl. in the mornynge.

god haue mercy vpon me. To whom the confeſſour ſayd. Nay I bad yᵉ ſay Agnus dei miſerere mei/ that is yᵉ lambe of god haue mercy vpon me.

Ye ſyr quod yᵉ penytent ye ſay trouth that was yᵉ laſte yere/ but now it is at twelfe month[2] ſyth/ & it is a ſhepe by this tyme. Therfore I muſt nedys ſay now yᵉ ſhepe of god haue mercy vpon me.

¶ By this tale ye may perceyue that yf holy ſcrypture be expownyd to rude[3] Lay people onely in the lytterall ſcence. Peraduenture it ſhal do but lytell[4] good.

LXVIII. ¶ *Of the huſband that ſayd he was John daw.*

T fourtuned dyuers to be in cõmunycacyon amonge whom there was a curat or a paryſh preeſt & one Johan daw a paryſhon of his whiche .ii. had cõmunycacyon more buſy than other in this maner. This preeſt thought yᵗ one myght not by felynge knowe one from another in the darke/ John

[2] *at twelfe month*] Hazl. a twelfemonthe.
[3] *rude*] Hazl. the.
[4] *but lyttel*] Hazl. lytell.

daw his paryſhon of contrary¹ opynyon layde with his curate for a wager .xl. pence.

Wherupon the paryſh preeſt wyllynge to proue his wager wente to this John dawes houſe in the euenynge and ſodenly gate hym to bed with his wyfe where whē he began to be ſomwhat beſy. She felynge his crowne ſayde ſhortly with a loud voyce. By god thou art not John daw. That herynge her huſbond anſwerde. Thou ſayſt trouth wyfe I am here John daw. Therfore mayſter perſon gyue me the money for you haue loſt your .xl. pence.

¶ By this tale ye may lerne to perceyue y^t it is no wyſdome for a man for ye couetouſe of wynnyng of any wager to put in Jeoperdy a thyng that may torne hym to gretter dyſplaſure.

LXIX. ¶ *Of the ſkoler of oxford that prouyd by ſoupheſtry .ii. chekyns .iii.*

In Ottom. Luſcinius, "Joci ac Sales, &c." 1524, No. 36, three eggs are proved to be five; ſee "Certayne Conceyts and Jeaſts," 1614, No. 32, in "Shakeſpeare Jeſt-Books," iii. p. 14; in Joh. Manlius, "Loci Communes," Baſil. 1590, p. 451, three eggs to be ſix; repeated in Joh. Pet. de Memel,

¹ *of contrary*] Hazl. of the contrary.

"Luſtige Geſellſchaft," 1695, No. 609. Cammerer, "Fabulæ Æſopicæ," Lips. 1570, p. 384, has a ſtory where two eggs are made ſix; in Gerlach, "Eutrapeliarum," lib. i. No. 871, p. 227, (Lips. 1656,) four eggs are made ſeven. Similar ſtories in Mart. Montanus, "Gartengeſellſchaft," Strafsb. s. a. 14; in "Scoggin's Jeſts," 1626, Mr. Hazlitt's reprint, p. 62; and in "Joake upon Joake," 1721. Compare Cénac Moncaut, "Contes Populaires de la Gaſcogne," Paris, 1861, p. 5; Reinh. Koehler in "Jahrbuch für Romaniſche und Engliſche Literatur," ed. by Ebert, vol. v. faſc. 1, p. 4.

 RYCH frankelyn in yᵉ contrey hauynge by his wyfe but one chyld and no mo for the grete affeccyon that he had to his ſayde chylde founde hym at Oxford to ſcole by the ſpace of .ii. or .iii. yere. This yonge ſcoller in a vocacyon tyme for his dyſport came home to his fader.

It fortuned afterwarde in[2] a nyght the fader yᵉ moder & the ſayde yonge ſcoller ſyttynge at ſupper hauynge before them no more mete but onely a cople of chykyns the fader ſayd this wyfe. Sone ſo it is that I haue ſpent moch money vpon the to fynde yᵉ to ſcole/ wherfore I haue grete deſyre to know what haſt lernyd. To whom yᵉ ſone anſwerde & ſayde. Fader I haue ſtudyed foueſtrye & by that ſcyence I can proue y theſe

[2] *in*] Hazl. on.

.ii. chykyns in yᵉ dyſh be thre chykyns. Mary ſayd yᵉ fader that wolde I fayne ſe. The ſcoller toke one of yᵉ chykyns in his hand & ſayd. Lo here is one chykyn/ and incõtynent he toke both yᵉ chykyns in his hand ioyntly & ſayd here is .ii. chykyns and one & .ii. maketh .iii. Ergo here is .iii. chykyns. Then the fader toke one of the chykyns to hymſelfe and gaue another to his wyfe & ſayd thus. Lo I wyll haue one of yᵉ chykyns to my parte/ & thy moder ſhall haue another & bycauſe of thy good argument thou ſhalt haue yᵉ thyrde to thy ſupper/ for thou getteyſt no more mete here at this tyme/ whiche promyſe the fader kept & ſo the ſcoller went without his ſupper.

¶ By this tale men may ſe that it is grete foly to put one to ſcole to lerne any ſubtyll ſcyence whiche hath no naturall wytte.

LXX. ¶ *Of the frere that ſtale the podyng.*

The ſame ſtory is found in Tarlton's "Jeſts and News out of Purgatory," 1590, edited by J. O. Halliwell, Lond. 1844, (Shakeſpeare Society,) p. 82.

FRERE of london there was that on a ſondaye mornynge yarly in yᵉ ſomer ſeaſõ came from Londõ to Barnet to make a colacyon/[1] & was there an houre before hye maſſe began/ & bycauſe he wolde come to yᵉ chyrch honeſtly/ he went fyrſt to an alehouſe there to wype his ſhoys & to make hymſelf clenely. In the which houſe there were podyngis to ſelle/ & dyuers folkys there brekynge theyr faſte & etyng podyngys. But yᵉ frere brake his faſt in a ſecrete place in the ſame houſe.

This frere ſoone after came to the chyrch and by lycence of yᵉ curat enteryd in to the pulpet to make a colacyon or ſermon. And in his ſermon there he rebukyd ſore yᵉ maner of them that vſyd[2] to breke theyr faſt on the ſonday before hye maſſe & ſayd it was called yᵉ dyuyls blak brekfaſt. And with that worde ſpekyng as he dyd caſt his armys out to make his cõtenaũce there fell a podynge out of his ſleue/ which he hymſelf had ſtolẽ a lytel before in yᵉ ſame alehous & when yᵉ people ſawe that & ſpecyally they yᵗ brake theyr faſt there yᵉ ſame mornyng & knew wel that yᵉ wyfe had compleyned how ſhe had one of her podynges ſtolyn/ they laughyd ſo moche at the frere yᵗ he incõtynent went downe of the pulpet[3] for ſhame.

¶ By this tale a man may ſe that whẽ a precher

---

[1] *colacyon*] i. e. homily.
[2] *vſyd*] Hazl. met.
[3] *of the pulpet*] Hazl. out of the pulpet.

doth rebuke any fynne or vyce wherin he is knowẽ openly to be gylty hymſelf/ ſuche prechyng ſhall lytell edyfy to the people.

LXXI. *Of the frankelyns ſon that cam to take orders.*

To ſolve the ſame problem a wife aſks her huſband who had been the father of the miller's three ſons, whereupon this miller is proved to be the father of Shem, Ham, and Japheth, (Joh. Pet. de Memel, "Luſtige Geſellſchaft," 1695, 1.) In Gerlach, "Eutrapeliarum," lib. i. No. 665, p. 159, the queſtion is, who was the father of Zebedee's children, and the anſwer: our neighbour, Maſter Melcher, the miller; in "Scoggin's Jeſts," (repr. p. 68,) the ſcholar ſays, "Tom Miller of Oſeney was Jacob's father." Alſo in "Die Sutorio Magiſtrale ſeltzame Metamorphoſis (der Pedantiſche Jrrthum, &c." Rapperſweil, 1673), and in Balthaſar Schupp (Wackernagel's "Leſebuch," iii. 795.)

A very ſimilar ſtory can be heard to this day in Germany: A waiter in the Weidenbuſch Hotel in Frankfort o. M. propoſes the following riddle to a Pruſſian Lieutenant: "It is not my brother, it is not my ſiſter, and yet it is my mother's child." The lieutenant gueſſes and gueſſes, until at laſt the waiter tells him that it is he himſelf. On the following day the lieutenant puts the ſame riddle at an evening party. The whole company declares: "That is yourſelf, Lieutenant!" "No, Ladies and Gentlemen, it is the waiter at the Weidenbuſch Hotel."

CERTAYNE ſkoller ther was intendynge to be made preſt[1] whiche had nother grete wytte nor lernyng came to the byſshop to take orders/ whos folyſhneſſe yᵉ byſhop perceyuyng becauſe he was a ryche mānes ſon wolde not very ſtrongly oppoſe[2] hym but aſkyd hym this ſmall queſtyon. Noe had .iij. ſonnes/ Sem/ Cham & Japhet/ now tell me quod the byſshop wo was Japhetis father & thou ſhalt haue orders. Then ſayd yᵉ ſcoler By my trouth my lorde I pray you pardō me. For I neuer lernyd but lyttel of the byble. Then quod the byſhop/ go home & come agayn & ſoyle me this queſtyon & thou ſhalt haue orders.

This ſcoler ſo departed & came home to his fader & ſhewde hym yᵉ cauſe of the hynderaunce of his orders.

His fader beynge angry at his folyſshnes thought to teche hym yᵉ ſolucyon of this queſtyon by a famylyer example & called his ſpanyels before hym & ſayd thus/ thou knowyſt well Coll my dogge hath theſe iii. whelpys Ryg/ Tryg/ & Tryboll. Muſt not Coll my dog[3] nedys be Syre to tryboll. Then quod the ſcoler by god fader

---

[1] *preſt*] Hazl. a preeſt.
[2] *oppoſe*] in orig. appoſe.
[3] *Coll my dog*] Hazl. all my dogges.

ye faye trouth let me alone now/ ye fhall fe me do well ynough yᵉ nexte tyme. wherfore on yᵉ morowe he wente to yᵉ byfshop agayne & fayd he coud foyle his queftyon. Then fayd the byfshop Noe had .iii. fonnes Sem Cham & Japhet/ now tell me who was Japhetys fader. Mary fyr quod yᵉ fcoler yf it pleafe your lordfhyp Col my faders dog.

¶ By this tale a man may lerne that it is but loft tyme to teche a fole any thynge whych hath no wyt to perceyue it.

LXXII. *Of the hufbandman that lodgyd the frere in hys owne bed.*

IT fortuned fo that a frere late in the euenynge defyred lodgynge of a poore man of the countrey/ the whiche for lake of other lodgynge glad to herborowe the frere lodgyd hym in his owne bed. And after he and his wyfe. The frere beynge a fleepe came and lay in the fame bedde.

And in the mornynge after the poore man rofe and wente to the marketh leuynge the Frere in yᵉ bedde with his wyfe. And as he went he fmylyd & laughyd to hymfelf/ wherfor his neybours demaunded of hym why he fo fmyled/ he answerd & fayd I laugh to thynk how fhamefaft the frere fhall be when he waketh/ whom I left in bedde with my wyfe.

¶ By this tale a man may lerne that he that ouerfhotyth hymfelf doth folyfhly yet he is more fole to fhewe it openly.

LXXIII. *Of the preft that wold fay .ii. gofpels for a grote.*

A very curious inftance of a corruption proving an edition to be a revifion of an older text. Mr. Hazlitt reads "fhorte fpace," and there can be no doubt, that our reading, "fhoterey," is the original and older one, as a village, Shottery, is fituated, exactly as our ftory mentions, not a mile from Stratford-on-Avon (Weft), between this place and Bordon Hill.

SOMTYME there dwellyd a preft in Stretforth vpon auyne of fmall lernynge whiche vndeuoutly fange maffe/ & often tymes twyfe on one day. So it happened on a tyme after his fecõde mas was done in fhoterey[1] not a myle from Strethforth there mete with hym dyuers merchaunt men whiche wolde haue harde maffe/ & defyryd hym to fynge maffe and he fholde haue a grote/ whiche anfwerd them

---

[1] *fhoterey*] Hazl. fhorte fpace.

& fayd Syrs I wyll fay maffe no more this day/ but I wyl fay you .ii. gofpels for one grote/ & that is dog chepe a maffe in ony place in englonde.

¶ By this tale a man may fe that they that be rude & vnlernyd regard but lytell the meryt & goodnes of holy prayer.

LXXIV. *Of the courtear that dyd caft the frere ouer the bote.*

Too imperfect to decypher in Hazl.

A COURTYER & a frere happenyd to mete togyder in a fery bote & in cōmunycacyon betwene them fell at wordys angry & dyfpleafyd eche with other/ & fought & ftrogled togyder/ fo that at the laft ye courtyer caft the frere ouer the bote/ fo was ye frere drowned. The feryma͂ whiche had ben a man of warre the moft parte of his lyfe before and feynge the frere was fo drowned & gon fayd thus to the courtyer/ I befhrewe thy hart thou fholdeft haue taryed & foughte with hym a lande for nowe thou haft caufed me to lefe an halfpeny for my fare.

¶ By this tale a man may fe that he yt is ac-
coftumed in vycyous & cruel company fhall lofe
that noble vertew to haue pyte & compaffyon
vpon his neyghboure.

LXXV. *Of the frere that prechyd what mennys
fowlys were.*

PRECHER in the pulpet[1] whiche
prechyd the worde of god/ & amõg
other matters fpake of mennys foullys
& fayd they were fo meruelous & fo fubtyll yt
a thoufand foullys myght daūce in the fpace of a
nayle of a mannys fynger/ amonge whiche audyence there was a mery conceyted felowe of
fmall deuocyon that anfwerde and fayd thus/
mayfter doctor yf that[2] a thoufande foullys may
daunce on a mannys nayle I pray you tell then[3]
where fhall the pyper ftande.

¶ By this tale a man may fe that it is but foly
to fhewe or to teche vertew to them that haue
no pleafure nor mynde therto.

[1] *in the pulpet*] Hazl. in pulpet.
[2] *yf that*] Hazl. yf.
[3] *you tell then*] Hazl. you than.

LXXVI. *Of the huſband that cryed ble vnder the bed.*

This tale, the origin of which perhaps may go back to Oriental ſources, (ſee Theodor Benfey, " Pantſchatantra," Leipzig, 1859, vol. ii. p. 258,) is taken from the " Cent Nouvelles Nouvelles," nov. 4; it is repeated in Celio Maleſpini, " Ducento Novelle," nov. 15, and in " Les joyeuſes Adventures et nouvelles Récréations," Paris, 1682, p. 35, 5to, devis 9.

N londõ there was a certayn artyfycer hauyng a wyf to whõ a luſty galãt made purſute to accomplyſhe his pleaſur. This womã denyenge ſhewde the matter vnto her huſbande/ whiche mouyd therwith bad hys wyfe to appoynte hym a tyme to come ſecretly to lye with her all night. And w^t gret krakys & othes ſware y^t agaynſt his coming he wolde be redy harneſyd & wolde put hym in ieopardy of his lyf except[1] he wolde make hym a grete amendys. This nyght was then[2] appoynted at whiche tyme this courtyer came at

---

[1] *agaynſt hys coming . . . of his lyf except*] This paſſage is apparently corrupt in orig., it reads: agaynſt his lyf except coming . . . in jeopardy of his comyng, he wolde, &c.

[2] *then*] orig. reads them.

his howre & entred into the chaumber[3] fet[4] his two handfworde[5] downe & fayde thefe wordes. Stand thou there thou fworde the deth of .iii.[6] men.

This hufbande lyenge vnder ye bed in harnes heryng thefe wordes lay ftyl for fere. The courtyer anone gat him to bed with the wyfe aboute his prepenfyd befynes/ and within an houre or .ii.[7] the hufbande beynge wery of lyenge began to remoue hym/ the courtyar that herynge afkyd the wyfe what thynge that was y^t remouyd vnder ye bed/ whiche excufynge ye matter fayde it was a lytell fhepe that was wonte dayly to go about the hous & the hufbande y^t herynge anone cryed ble as it had ben a fhepe.

And fo in cōclufyon when ye courtyer faw his tyme he rofe & kyffed the wyfe & toke his leue & departyd. And as foone as he was gone the hufbande arofe/ & when the wyfe lokyd on hym fomwhat abaffhyd fhe began to make a fad coūtenaunce & fayde Alas fyr why dyd ye not ryfe & play the man as ye fayde ye wolde/ whiche anfwerde and fayde why dame dydeft thou not here hym fay that his fworde had ben the dethe

[3] *into the chaumber*] Hazl. in at the chamber.
[4] *fet*] Hazl. and fet.
[5] *two handfworde*] Hazl. two-hande fworde.
[6] .*iii.*] Hazl. thre. [7] .*ii.*] Hazl. two.

of .iii. men/ & I had ben a fole than yf y^t I had put my felfe in ieopardy to haue ben the fourth. Then fayd the wyfe thus/ but fyr fpake not I wyfely then when I fayd ye were a fhepe/ yes quod ye hufbande. But than dyd not I more wyfely dame when that I cryed ble.

¶ By this ye may fe that he is not wyfe that wyll put his confydens to moche vpon thefe grete crakers whiche oftymes wyll do but lytell when it comyth to the poynt.

LXXVII. *Of the fhomaker that afkyd the colyer what tydyngys in hell.*

A correfponding tale in Lyrum Carum, 125.

THERE was a fhomaker[1] fyttynge in his fhop y^t fawe a colyer come by thought to deryde hym bycaufe he was fo blake/ afkyd[2] hym what thydynges were in hell[3] and how the deuyll fayred. To whome the colyer fayde/ the deuyll fared well[4] when

[1] *There was a fhomaker*] Hazl. A fouter.
[2] *afkyd*] Hazl. and afked.
[3] *what thydynges were in hell*] Hazl. what newes from hell.
[4] *fayde/ the deuyll fared well*] Hazl. anfwered hym he was well.

I ſawe hym laſt for he was rydynge forthe and taryed but for a ſowter⁵ to pluk on his botis.

¶ By this ye may ſe that he that vſyth to deryde other folkys is ſomtyme hymſelfe more derydyd and mokkyd.

LXXVIII. *Of ſeynt Peter that cryed cauſe bobe.*

FYNDE wrytẽ amonge olde geſtys how god made ſaynte peter porter of heuen/ and that god of his goodnes ſoone after his paſſyon ſuffred many men to come to the kyngdome of heuen with ſmall deſeruyng/ at whiche tyme there was in heuen a grete company of Welchemen/ whiche with theyre krakynge & babelynge trobelyd all the other. Wherfore god ſayd to ſaynt peter yᵗ he was wery of them/ & that he wolde fayne haue them out of heuen. To whome ſaynt Peter ſayde good lorde I warrant you yᵗ ſhalbe ſhortly done/⁶ wherfore ſaynt peter went out of heuẽ gatys & cryed wᵗ a loude voyce Cauſe bobe/ yᵗ is as moche to ſay as roſtyd cheſe/ whiche thynge yᵉ welchmen heryng ran out of heuyn a great pace. And when ſaynt Peter ſawe them al out he ſodenly went in to

---

⁵ *ſowter*] i. e. cobbler. ⁶ *ſhortly done*] Hazl. done.

heuen and lokkyd the dore and ſo ſparryd all the welchmen out.

¶ By this ye may ſe that it is no wyſdome for a man to loue or to ſet his mynde to moche vpon ony delycate or wordly pleaſure wherby he ſhall loſe the celeſtyall & eternall Joye.

LXXIX. *Of hym that aduenturyd body & ſowle for hys prynce.*

TWO knyghtes there were whiche went to a ſtondyng felde wᵗ theyr prynce. But one of them was cõfeſſyd before he went/ but the other wẽt into the felde w'out ſhryft or repẽtaũce/ afterward this prĩce wã yᵉ feld & had yᵉ vyctorye yᵗ day/ wherfore he yᵗ was cõfeſſyd came to yᵉ prĩce & aſkyd an offyce & ſayd he had deſeruyd¹ it for he had don good ſeruyce & aduẽtured that day as far as ony man in yᵉ felde/ to whõ the other yᵗ was vncõfeſſyd anſweryd and ſayd nay by the mas I am more worthy to haue a rewarde than he/ for he ad-uenturyd but his body for your ſake for he durſt not go to yᵉ felde tyl he was cõfeſſyd/ but as for

---

¹ *he had deſeruyd*] Hazl. that he had deſerved.

MERY TALYS. 133

me I dyd iupd both body lyfe & foule for your fake/ for I went to the felde without cõfeſſyon or repentañce.

LXXX. *Of the parſon that ſtall the mylners elys.*

Too imperfect to decypher in Hazl.
In Reginald Scot, " Diſcovery of Witchcraft," 1584, London, 1651, 4to. p. 191, the ſame ſtory is related.

CERTAYN mylner ther was which had dyuers põdys of elis wherĩ was good ſtore of elys/ wherfore yᵉ pſon of yᵉ town which lokyd like ã holy mã dyuers & many timis ſtale many of thẽ in ſo moch yᵗ he had left few or none behind him/ wherfore this milner ſeyng his elis ſtolyn & wiſt not by whõ cam to yᵉ ſayd pſon & deſyrid² hym to curſe for thẽ yᵉ pſon ſayd he wolde. & yᵉ next sõday cã in to yᵉ pulpet wᵗ book bell & cãdell & pceiyng there were none in yᵉ chirche yᵗ vnderſtode latyn ſayd thus/ he yᵗ ſtale yᵉ milners elis laudate dominum de celis but he yᵗ ſtale yᵉ grer elis gaudeat ipſe in celis/ therwᵗ put out yᵉ candell. why³ ſyr quod yᵉ mylner no more for this ſauce is ſharp ynough for hym.

² *deſyrid*] in orig. deſtrid.   ³ *why*] in orig. who.

¶ By this ye may ſe that ſome curatys that loke full holyly be but deſemblers & ypocrytis.

LXXXI. *Of the welchman that ſaw one .xl. ſhyl. better than god.*

 WELCHMAN on a tyme went to chirche to here mas whiche hapenyd to come in euyn at yᵉ ſacryng time when he had hard yᵗ mas to yᵉ ende he wēt home wher one of his felowes aſkyd hym whether he had ſene god almighty to day which āſwerd & ſayd nay but I ſaw one lx. s. better thā he.

¶ By this ye maye ſe that they be euyll brought vp haue but lytyll devocyon to pray and vertew.[1]

LXXXII. *Of the frere that ſayd dyrige for the hoggys ſowle.*

A correſponding tale is found in the "Nouveaux Contes à rire," &c. Cologne, 1702, p. 13: "Cochon adroitement volé par des Bohémiens," where a family of thieves ſteal a hog, kill it, and upon ſearch being made for it, cover it with a cloth and weep as for their father.

[1] The moral is wanting in Hazl.

UPON a tyme certayn women in the countrey were appoynted to deryde and mokke a frere a lymytour that vſyd moche to vyſyth them. wherupon one of them a lytyll before that[2] the frere came kylled an hog & for dyſport leyd[3] it vnder the borde after the maner of a corſe and tolde the frere it was her good mã and deſyred hym to ſay dirige for his ſoule wherfore the frere and his felaw began Placebo and Dirige and ſo forth ſayd the ſeruyſe full deuowtly which the wyues ſo heryng/ coude not refrayne them ſelfe from lawghynge and wente in to a lytyll parler to lawgh more at theyr pleſure. Theſe frerys ſomwhat ſuſpected the cauſe and quykly or that ye women were ware lokyd vnder the borde and ſpyed that it was an hog/ ſodenly toke it bytwene them and bare it homeward as faſt they myght.[4] The women ſeyng that ran after the frere and cryed come agayn mayſter frere come agayne and let it allone/ nay by my fayth quod ye frere he is a broder of oures and therfore he muſt nedys be buryed in our cloyſter/ and ſo the frerys gate the hog.

    [2] *before that*] Hazl. before.
    [3] *leyd*] in orig. ſeyd.
    [4] *as faſt they myght*] Hazl. as faſt as they might.

¶ By this ye may ſe that they that vſe to deryde and mok other ſomtyme it tornyth to theyr one loſſe and damage.

LXXXIII. *Of the parſon that ſayd maſſe of requiē for Cryſtys ſowle.*

This tale is taken from Henr. Bebelii, "Facetiæ, Opuſ-cula," s. l. & a. 4to. ſign. A a 4, "Fabula," (or in Friſch-lini, "Facet." i. No. 7, p. 37, "De inſcitia cuiusdam ſacerdotis fabula perfaceta"): "Neſciebat quidam ſacerdos ſatis inſulſus, quid eſſet cantandum in officio diuino die reſurrectionis chriſtianæ, miſit itaque ædituum ad vicinum ſacerdotem, qui cum dixiſſet, Reſurrexi, ædituus literarum ignarus, tantum meminit re, quod ſæpius repetiuit, quo audito ſacerdos ille ſimplex et rudis, bene eſt, dixit requiem cantandum eſt, quoniam diem depoſitionis (vt vocant) Jeſu Chriſti celebrari convenit, nam in triduo mortuus eſt."

It is repeated in "Der Wegkürzer, das dritte theil des Rollwagens," &c. Frankf. 1590, fol. 15 *verſo;* and in "Scoggin's Jeſts," 1626, p. 74, (repr. 1864, p. 75,) "How the Prieſt ſaid *Requiem æternam* on Eaſter day."

CERTAYNE preſt there was that dwellyd in yᵉ coūtery which was not very¹ lernyd. Therfore on Eeſter euyn he ſēt his boy to yᵉ preſt of the next town

---

¹ *very*] Hazl. very well.

yᵗ was .ii. myle from thens to know what maſſe he ſholde ſynge on yᵉ morowe. This boy came to the ſayd preſt and did his mayſters errāde to hym. Then quod the preſt tel thy mayſter that he muſt ſynge to morow of the reſurrexyon/ and furthermore quod he yf thou hap to forget it tel thy mayſter that it begynneth wᵗ a gret R. and ſhewed hym the maſſe booke where it was wryten Reſurrexi. &c. This boy than wente home agayne and all the way as he went he clateryd ſtyll. Reſurrexi Reſurrexi/ but at yᵉ laſt he hapenyd to forget it clene and whē he came home his mayſter aſkyd hym what maſſe he ſholde ſynge on yᵉ morowe. By my troth mayſter quod the boy I haue forgoten it/ but he bad me tell you it begā wᵗ a gret .R. By god quod the preſt I trowe thou ſayeſt trowth for now I remember well it muſte be requiem eternam/ for god almyghty dyed as on yeſter day² & now we muſt ſay maſſe for his ſoule.

¶ By this ye may ſe that when one fole ſendyth another fole on his errand oftentymes the beſynes is folyſhly³ ſpede.

  ² *as on yeſter day*] Hazl. upon Good Fryday.
  ³ *is folyſhly*] Hazl. folyhly.

LXXXIV. *Of the herdman that ſayd ryde apace ye ſhall haue rayn.*

In "Joe Miller's complete Jeſt Book," London, 1845, No. 425, p. 128, the ſame ſtory is told of Newton. See "Scoggin's Jeſts," 1796, p. 47: "How Scogin gave a Cowheard forty ſhillings to teach him his cunning in the weather." Mr. Hazlitt's reprint, p. 115.

SKOLER of Oxenford whiche had ſtudyed yᵉ iudycyals of aſtronomy õ a tyme was rydyng by yᵉ way which cã by a herdmã & inquyrid of hym how far it was to yᵉ next town/ ſyr quod yᵉ herdmã ye haue notthyder paſt a myle & ã half/ but ſyr quod he ye nede to ryde apace for ye ſhal haue a ſhour of rayn er ye cõe thyder/ what quod yᵉ ſkoler yᵗ is not ſo for here is no token of rayn for all¹ yᵉ cloudys be both fayr & clere/ by god ſyr quod yᵉ herd mã but ye ſhall fynd it ſo. The ſkoler then rode forth his way & or he had ryden half a myle forther there fel a good ſhowre of rayn that the ſkoler was well waſhyd and wete to yᵉ ſkyn/ yᵉ ſkoler then tournyd his horſe and rode agayne² to the herdman & deſyred hym to teche hym that connyng. nay quod yᵉ herdman I wyll

---

¹ *for all*] Hazl. for.   ² *rode agayne*] Hazl. rode.

not teche you my connynge for nought/ thã the
ſkoler profferyd hym .xl. ſhyllyngys to teche hym
that connynge/ the herde man after he had re-
ceyued his money ſayde thus. Syr ſe you not yõder
dun a kow³ with the whyte face/ yes quod the
ſkoler. Suerly quod yᵉ herdmã whẽ ſhe daũſyth
and holdyth vp her tayle it ſhal haue a ſhowre of
rayne within halfe an howre after.

¶ By this ye may ſee yᵗ the cõnyng of herdmen⁴
& ſhepardes as touchyng alteracyõs of weders
is more ſure than yᵉ iudycyallys of Aſtronomy.

LXXXV. *Of hym that ſayd I ſhall haue nere
a peny.*

IN a certayn town ther was a rych man
that lay on his deth bed at poynte of
deth whiche chargyd his executours
to dele⁵ for his ſoule a certayn ſõme of money
in pence & on this condicyon chargyd them as
yᵉ wolde anſwere afore God⁶ that euery pore
man that came to them & tolde a trewe tale
ſholde haue a peny & they that ſayd a fals

---

³ *kow*] Hazl. ewe.
⁴ *herdmen*] orig. reads herdman.
⁵ *to dele*] i. e. to give.
⁶ *afore God*] in orig. afore. God.

thynge sholde haue none/ & in the dole¹ tyme there came one which sayde y^t god was a good man/ quod ye executours thou shalt haue a peny for thou sayste trouth. Anone came another & said ye deuyll was a good man/ quod the executours there thou lyest therfore thou shalt haue nere a peny. At last came one to ye executours & sayd thus/ ye shall gyue me nere a peny/ which wordys made the executours amasyd and toke aduysement whether they shold gyue hym the peny or no.

¶ By this ye may se it is wysdome for Juggys in deutefull matters of law to beware of hasty iugement.

LXXXVI. *Of the husband that sayd his wyfe and he agreed well.*

Too imperfect to decypher in Hazl.

A MAN askyd his neybour which was but late maryed to a wydow how he agreyd with his wyfe for he said y^t her fyrst husbãd and she coud neuer agre/ by god quod ye other we agre meruelous wel. I pray the how so/ mary quod ye other I shall tell y^e/

¹ *dole*] i.e. grief.

when I am mery fhe is mery/ & when I am fad fhe is fad/ for whẽ I go out of my doris I am mery to go from her & fo is fhe/ & when I come in agayne I am fad & fo is fhe.

LXXXVII. *Of the preeft that fayd comede epifcope.*

From the " Margarita Facetiarum," Argent. 152, fign. O vi.

Another verfion of this tale is related in " Scoggin's Jefts:" How the Prieft was complained on for keeping a young wench in his houfe," (repr. 1864, p. 78.)

IN yᵉ tyme of vyfytacyõ a bysfhop whiche was fomwhat lecherous & had got many chylderne preparyd to come to a preftes houfe to fe [2] what rule he kept which preft had a lemã in his houfe called Ede & by her had .ii. or .iii. fmale chyldrẽ in fhort fpace/ but agayn yᵉ bysfhop commyng yᵉ preft [3] preparyd a rome to hyde his lemã & his childrẽ ouer in yᵉ rofe of his hall/ & whẽ yᵉ bysfhop was come & fet at dyner in yᵉ fame hal hauyng .x. of his owne childrẽ about hym this prefte which coud fpeke lytell latyn or none bad the bysfhop in

---

[2] *to come to a preftes houfe to fe*] Hazl. to queftion a preeft.

[3] *the preft*] Hazl. he.

latyn to ete faynge Comede epifcope. This womã in the rofe of the houfe herynge the preft fay fo had wente he had callyd her byddynge her com Edee & ãfwerd fhortly & fayd fhall I brynge my chylderen w^t me alfo. This byffhop herynge this[1] vxor tua ficut vitis abundans in lateribus domus tue. The preeft thẽ half amafyd anfweryd fhortly[2] and fayd Filii tui ficut nouelle[3] olyuarum in circuitu menfe tue.

¶ By this ye may fe that they that haue but fmall lernynge fomtyme fpeke truely vnaduyfyd.

LXXXVIII. *Of the woman that ftale the pot.*

ON afhe wednyfday in ye mornynge was a curat of a church whiche had made good chere the nyght afore/ & fyttyn vp late & came to ye churche to here cõfeffyon to whom there came a woman/ and amõge other thyngys fhe cõfeffyd her that fhe had ftolyn a pot. But than becaufe of grete watche that this preeft had/ he there fodenly felle a flepe/ and whẽ this woman fawe hym not wyllyng to here her fhe rofe vp[4] & wẽt her way/ & anone an

---

[1] *herynge this*] Hazl. hering this, fayde in fporte.
[2] *anfweryd fhortly*] Hazl. anfwerd.
[3] *nouelli*] orig. reads nouelle.
[4] *rofe vp*] Hazl. rofe.

other woman kneled downe to the fame preſt & began to ſay benedicite wherwith this preeſt ſodenly wakyd wenynge⁵ ſhe had ben the other woman & ſayd al angerly/ what art thou now at benedicite agayne tell me what dydeſt thou when thou hadyſt ſtolyn the pot.

LXXXIX. *Of maſter whyttyntons dreme.*

SONE after one mayſter Whyttintõ had bylded a colege on a nyght as he ſlept he dremyd that he ſad in his church & many folkys ther alſo/ & further he dremyd yᵗ he ſawe our lady in the ſame chyrch wᵗ a glas of goodly oyntement in her hand goynge to one aſkyng hym what he had done for her ſake/ whiche ſayd that he had ſayd our ladys ſauter⁶ euery day wherfore ſhe gaue hym a lytyll of the oyle. And anon ſhe went⁷ to another aſkyng hym what he had done for her ſake which ſayd that he had ſayd .ii. ladys ſauters euery day/ wherfore our lady gaue hym more of yᵉ oỹtement than ſhe gaue yᵉ other. This mayſter whyttentõ

---

⁵ *wakyd wenynge*] Hazl. awaked, and wenynge.
⁶ *ſauter*] i. e. Pſalter.
⁷ *ſhe went*] in orig. ſe went.

then thought that when our lady sholde come to hym she wolde gyue hym all the hole glas bycaufe y^t he had bylded fuch a gret colege & was very glad in his mynd. But whẽ our lady cam to hym she afked hym what he had fuffred for her fake/ which wordys made hym gretly abafhyd bycaufe he had nothyng to fay for hym felfe/ & fo he dremyd¹ that for all the gret dede of byldyng of ye fayd Colege he had no parte of y^t goodly oyntement.

¶ By this ye may² fe that to fuffer for goddys fake is more merytoryous than to gyue gret goodys.

 xc. *Of the preft that kyllyd hys horfe callyd modicum.*

CERTAYNE byfshop appoynted to go on vyfytacyon to a preftys hous³ and bycaufe he wolde haue the preeft do but lytell⁴ coft vpon hym he bad hym dreffe⁵ but lytyl mete faying thus in latyn.⁶ Preparas

 ¹ *he dremyd*] Hazl. him informed.
 ² *may*] orig. reads mnay.
 ³ *preftys hous*] Hazl. preefte's.
 ⁴ *lytell*] in orig. lyiell.
 ⁵ *bad hym dreffe*] Hazl. told him to prepare.
 ⁶ *thus in latyn*] Hazl. thus.

mihi modicū. This preeſt which vnderſtode hym not halfe wel had a horſe called modicū wherfore he thought to obtayne the bysſhops fauour & agaynſt ye bysſhops comyng kylled his horſe that was called modicum wherof the byſſop & his ſeruātes ete pt which whē ye bisſhop knew afterward was gretly diſpleſid.

¶ By this ye may ſe that many a fole doth moche coſt which[7] hath but lytyll thank for his laboure.

XCI. *Of the maltman of Colbroke.*

Wanting in Hazl.
Similar trickeries are of very frequent occurrence; ſee f. i. Kirchhof, "Wendunmuth," Frankf. 1573, No. 313-17, fol. 302 *verſo*.

CERTAYNE maltman of colbroke whiche was a very couetous wreche and had no pleaſure but onely to get money came to london to ſell his malt and broughte with hym .iiii. capons & there reſeyuyd .iiii. or .v. li. for malte and put it in a lytell purs tyed to his cote and after wente aboute the ſtrettys to ſell his capons whom a pollyng

---

[7] *which*] Hazl. at dyners, whiche.

felowe that was a dycer and an vnthryft had efpyed and Imagyned how he myght begyle the man other of his capons or of his money and came to this maltman in the ftreet berynge thefe capons in his hande and afkyd hym how he wolde fell his capons and when he had fhewyd hym the pryfe of them he bad hym go with hym to his mayfter and he wolde fhew them to his mayfter and he wolde caufe hym to haue money for them wherto he agreed. This Poller wente to the cardynalls hat in lomberdys ftrete & when he came to the dore he toke the capons from the maltman and bad hym tary at the dore tyll he had fhewed his mayfter and he wolde come agayn to hym and brynge hym his money for them. This poller when he had goten the capons wente in to the houfe and wente thorowe the other bak entre in to Cornhyll and foo toke the capons with hym/ and when this maltman had ftond there a good feafon he afkid one of the tauerners where the man was that had the Capons to fhewe to his mayfter/ mary quod the tauerner I can not tell the here is nother mayfter nor man in this houfe for this entre here is a comen hye way and gooth in to cornhyl/ I am fure he is gone a weye with thy capõs. This maltman herynge that ran throwe the entre in to cornhyll and afkyd for a felowe in a tawny cote that had capons in his

hand. But no man coude tell hym whiche waye
he was gone and ſoo the maltman loſte his capons
and after wente in to his Inne all heuy and ſade
and toke his horſe to thentent to ryde home.
This poller by that tyme had chaungyd hys rayment and borowyd a furryd gowne and came to
the maltman ſyttynge on horſbak and ſayd thus/
good man me thought I harde the inquire euyn
now for one in a tawny cote that had ſtolyn from
the .iiii. capōs yf thou wylt gyue me a quart of
wyne go with me and I ſhall brynge y^e to a place
where he ſyttyth drynkyng with other felowes
& had ye capons in his hande. This maltman
beynge glad therof graūtyd hym to gyue hym
the wyne bycauſe he ſemyd to be an honeſt man/
and went w^t hym vnto the dagger in chepe.
This poller then ſayd to hym go thy way ſtreyght
to thend of y^t long entre & there thou ſhalt ſe
whether it be he or no & I wyl holde thy horſe
here tyll thou come agayn. This maltman
thynkyng to fynde the felow with his capōs
wēt in & left his horſe with the other at the
dore. And as ſoone as he was gon in to the
houſe this poller lad the horſe awaye in to his
owne lodgynge. This maltman inqueryd in the
houſe for his felowe with the capons but no man
coude tell hym no tydyngys of ſuche man/ wherfore he came agayne to ye dore all ſad & lokyd

for hym y^t had his hors to kepe/ & bycaufe he fawe hym not he afkyd dyuers there for hym/ & fome fayd they faw hym & fome fayde they faw hym not/ but no man coude tell whiche waye he was gone wherfore he wente home to his Inne more fad thã he was before/ wherfore his hoft gaue hym coūcell to get hym home & beware how he truftyd any men in londõ. This maltman feynge none other cõfort went hys hy way homewarde.

This poller which lyngeryd alway there aboute the Inne hard tell that the maltman was goyng homewarde a fote apparelyd hym lyke a mannys prentyfe & gat a lytell boget ftuffyd full of ftones on his bake & wente before hym to charynge croffe & taryed tyll ye maltman came/ & afkyd hym whether he wente whiche fayd to Colbroke. Mary quod ye other I am glad therof for I muft goo to braynforde to my mayfter to bere hym money which I haue in my boget & I wolde be glad of cõpany. This maltman bycaufe of his owne money was glad of his cõpany/ & fo they agreed & wente togyder a whyle. At the laft this poller went fomwhat before to knyghtbryge & fat vpon ye brydge & reftyd hym with his boget on his bak/ & when he faw ye maltmã almoft at hym he let his boget fall ouer ye brydge in to ye water. & incontynent ftart vp & fayd to ye maltman alas

I haue let my boget fal in to ye water & there is .xl. li. of money therin/ yf thou wylt wade in to ye water & go feke it & get it me agayne I fhall gyue y^e .xii. pence for thy labour/ this maltman hauynge pyte of his loffe & alfo glad to get the .xii. pence plukyd of his hofe cote & fhyrt & wadyd into ye water to feke for the boget. And in ye mene whyle this poller gote his clothis & cote wher to the purs of money was tyde & lepte ouer the hedge & wente to weftmynfter.

This maltman within a whyle after with grete payne & depe wadynge founde ye boget & came out of the water & fawe not his felowe there & fawe that his clothys & money were not there as he left them fufpectyd ye mater and openyd the boget and than founde nothynge therin but ftonys cryed out lyke a mad man and ran all nakyd to london agayne and fayde alas alas helpe or I fhall be ftolen. For my capons be ftolen. My hors is ftolen. My money and clothys be ftolen and I fhall be ftolen myfelf. And fo ran aboute the ftretys in london nakyd & mad cryenge alway I fhall be ftole. I fhall be ftolen. And fo contynuyd mad durynge his lyfe & fo dyed lyke a wretche to the vtter dyftruccyon of hym felf & fhame to all his kyn.

¶ By this tale ye may fe that many a couetoufe wrech y^t louyd his good better than god and settyth his mynde inordynatly theron by the ryghte iugment of god oftymes comyth to a myserable and shamfull ende.

xcii. *Of the welchman that stale the englyshmans cok.*

WELCHEMAN dwellynge in englonde fortuned to stele an englysh mans cok & sette it on yᵉ fyre to seth wherfore this englyshman suspectyng yᵉ welchmā cam in to his house¹ & sawe yᵉ cok setyng on yᵉ fyre & sayd to yᵉ welchmā thus. Syr this is my cok. Mary quod yᵉ welchmā & yf it be thyne yᵉ shalt haue thy parte of it/ nay quod yᵉ englyshmā yᵗ is not ynough. By cottes blut & her nayle quod yᵉ welchmā yf her be not ynough now her wyll be ynough anone for her hath a good fyre vnder her.

xciii. *Of hym that brought a botell to a prest.*

CERTAYNE of yᵉ vycars² of poulys dysposyd to be mery on a sondaye at hye masse tyme sent another mad felowe

---

¹ *in to his house*] Hazl. to his house.
² *of the vycars*] Hazl. vycars.

of theyr accoyntaūce vnto a folyſſhe dronken preſte to gyue hym a botell/ whiche man met with the preſte vpon the top of yᵉ ſtayrys by yᵉ chaūcell dore & ſpake to hym & ſayde thus. Syr my mayſter hath ſend you a botel to put your drynke in bycauſe ye can³ kepe none in your braynes. This preſte therwith beyng very angry all ſodenly toke the botell & with his fote flange⁴ it downe into yᵉ body of the chyrche vpon the gentylmens hedes.

xcɪv. *Of the endytemēt of Jheſu of Nazareth.*

 CERTAYNE Jury in the counte of Myddelſex was inpaneld for yᵉ kynge to inquere of all indytementes murders & felonyes. The perſons of this panel were folyſſhe couetous & vnlerned/ for who ſo euer wolde gyue thē a grote they wolde aſſyne & veryfy his byll whether it were true or fals w'out any other profe⁵ or euidēce/ wherfore one yᵗ was a mery cōceytyd felowe perceyuyng theyr ſmale cōcyence & grete couetouſnes put in a byll intytuled after this maner. Inquiratur pro dño regi

³ *ye can*] Hazl. he can.
⁴ *flange*] i. e. proje&t out.
⁵ *any other profe*] Hazl. any profe.

si Jesus nazarenus furatus est unū asinū ad equitandum in egiptū/ & gaue thē a grote and desyryd y^t it myght be veryfyed. The sayd Jury whiche loked all on the grote & nothyng on ye byll as was theyr vse wrote billa vera on ye bak therof which byll when it was presentyd into ye court whē ye Jugys loked theron they sayd opēly before all ye people lo fyrs here is ye meruelouſt verdyt y^t euer was presentyd by any[1] inquest for here they haue indyted Jesu of Nazareth for stelyng of an asse which whē ye people hard it/ it made thē both to laugh & to wōder at ye folyshnes & shāful piuri of thē of the equeste.

¶ By this ye may se it is grete parell to enpanell any iurorous[2] vpon any equest whiche be folysh & haue but small concyence.

xcv. *Of hym that prechyd agaynst theym that rode on the sonday.*

The same story is found in Frischlini, " Facetiæ," Lips. 1600 (or 1602), p. 2, De sacerdote jeiunium Quadragesimale defendente: " Quidam ineptus, ne dicam impius Sacerdos, cum jeiunium Quadragesimale et discrimen ciborum defenderet, et pœnam omnibus contemptoribus et hæreticis comminatus esset, ad erroris sui patrocinium etiam

[1] *any*] Hazl. an.
[2] *iurorous*] orig. reads iurroous.

Chrifti et Apoftolorum exemplo abutebatur. Quid enim, inquit, de Chrifto et Apoftolis eius dicam? qui nefcio qua voluptate deliniti, cum pafchatis fefto non expectato, die Jouis proxime antecedente, agnum deuoraffent, Chriftus ftatim altera poft die in crucem actus eft: Apoftolorum vero, qui vna comederant, nemo ficca morte perijt."

N a certayn paryfh a frere prechyd/ and in his fermon he rebuked them y^t rode on ye fonday/ euer lokyng vpon one man y^t was botyd & fpurryd redy to ryde. This man parceyuyng y^t all ye people notyt hym fodenly half in anger anfwerde ye frere thus/ why prechyft thou fo moch agaynft them y^t ryde on ye fonday for cryfte hymfelfe dyde ryde on palme sõday/ as thou knowyft well it is wryten in holy fcrypture. To whõ ye frere fodẽly anfwerd & fayd thus/ but I pray ye what cã therof was he not hãgid on ye fryday after/ which herynge all ye people in ye church fell on laughing.

XCVI. *Of the one brother that founde a purs.*

Repeated in "Joe Miller's Complete Jeft Book," London, 1845, No. 671, p. 205; and in Joh. Val. Meidinger, "Pract. Franzœfifche Grammatik," 23rd edit. (1818), p. 551. Comp. "Waldis, Æfopus," 4, 4.

THERE was a certayne man that had two fonnys vnlyke of condycyons. For the eldyft was lufty and quyk and vfyd moche to ryfe erly and walke in to the feldys/ than was the yonger flowe and vnlufty and vfyd to lye in bed[1] as longe as he myght. So on a daye the elder as he was wonte rofe erly and walkyd in to the feldys and there by fortune he founde a purs of money and brought it home to his fader. His fader when he had it wente ftreyght to his other fone yet lyenge then in his bed & fayd to hym. O thou flogarde quod he feyft thou not thyne elder[2] broder how he by his erly ryfyng had found a purs with money whereby we fhalby gretely holpen all oure lyfe/ whyle thou fluggynge in thy bed doft[3] no good but flepe. He then wyft not what to fay but anfweryd fhortly and fayd fader quod he yf he that hath loft the purs and money had lyne in his bed that fame tyme that he loft it as I do now my broder had founde no purs nor money to daye.

¶ By this ye may fe that they that be accuftomyd in vyce and fyn wyl alway fynd one excufe or other to cloke there with theyr vyce and vnthryftynes.

[1] *in bed*] Hazl. in his bed.   [2] *elder*] Hazl. eldeft.
[3] *doft*] Hazl. doft thou.

MERY TALYS. 155

XCVII. *Of the anſwere of the maſters to the mayd.*

CERTAYN wyfe ther was whiche was ſomwhat fayre and as all women be y*t* be y*e* fayre[4] was ſomwhat proude of her bewty/ & as ſhe and her mayd ſat togeder ſhe as one that was deſyrous to be preyſyd ſayd to her thus. I fayth Jone how tynkyſt thou am I not a fayre wyfe/ yes by my trouth mayſtres quod ſhe ye be the fayreſt that euer was except our lady/ why by Cryſt quod y*e* mayſtres though our lady were good yet ſhe was not ſo fayre as men ſpeke of.

¶ By this ye may ſe it is harde to fynde a bewtyouſe woman without pryde.

XCVIII. *Of a certayn aldermans dedys of london.*

Wanting in Hazl.

CERTAYNE alderman of London there was lately dyſceaſed whiche now ſhall be nameles whiche was very co-uetouſe as well before he was maryed as after/ for when he was bacheler euer when his hoſen were

[4] *the fayre*] Hazl. fayre.

broken so that he coude were them no longer for shame then wolde he cutte them of by the knee and putte on a payre of ledder buskyns on his bare leggys whiche wolde laste hym a two or thre yere. Furthermore it was his maner when he was a bacheler euery nyght where that he was to borowe a candels ende to brynge hym home whiche he wolde alway put in a chest that he had at his chamber. So that by that tyme he was maryed/ he had a cheste of candels endis that wayd two or thre hondred weyghte.

Sone after that he was maryed to a ryche wydowe and than folkys thought he wolde be better than he was before. But so it happenyd that a gentylman gaue hym a pasty of an harte whiche euery day he caused to be sette on the table for seruyce/ how be it he wolde neuer for nygynshyp let it be openyd/ so that it was a moneth or vi. wekys or euer it was touched. At whiche tyme it fortuned a man of his ac-coyneraunce beynge there often and seynge this pasty neuer to be openyd sayde syr by my trouth I wyll tame your pasty/ whiche openyd ye pasty and incontynent lepte out .iii. or .iiii. myce vpon other gentylmens trechows whiche had crept in at an hole vndernethe the bottam and hadde etyn vp all the mete therin. Also this alderman was of suche condycyon y^t he wolde here .ii. or .iii.

maſſys euery daye/ and whan any pore folke
came to begge of hym he wolde rebuke them
and ſay that they dyde lette hym in heryng of
them ſo that he wolde neuer gyue peny in almys.
And on a tyme as he ſat at ſaynt Thomas of
Acres herynge maſſe he ſawe a yonge begynner
a dettour of his that owyd hym .xx. li. whiche as
ſone as he ſawe hym he commaunded one of his
ſeruauntes to get a ſergyaunt & to areſt hym
whiche yonge man immedyatly after was areſtyd/
and whan he was in the counter he deſyred dyuers
of his frendys to intrete with this Aldermã for
dayes of payment whiche men in the mornynge
after came to this Alderman knelynge at maſſe
& intretyd hym for this man deſyrynge hym to
take dayes of paymẽt whiche anſweryd them
thus. I praye you troble me not now for I haue
harde one maſſe all redy & I wyll here an other
or I medle with worldly matters. But yf ye
haue the money here I wyll take the now or
elles I pray you ſpeke to me no more/ and ſo
theſe men coude get no other anſwer. And this
Alderman kept this yonge man ſtyll in pryſon
tyll at the laſte he there dyed. And ſo he cauſyd
lykewyſe dyuers other to dye in pryſon and wolde
neuer forgyue them/ wherfore afterward this alderman dyed ſodenly wherfore dyuers & many
were glad of his deth.

xcix. *Of the northern man that was all hart.*

A NORTHEN man there was whiche wente to ſeke hym a ſeruyce. So it happenyd that he came to a lordys place whiche lord than had war w^t another lord. This lord thã aſkyd this northẽ mã yf y^t he durſt fyght/ ye by goodys byẽs quod ye northẽ mã y^t I dare for I is al hart. whervpon the lorde retayned hym in to his ſeruyce. So after it happenyd y^t this lorde ſholde go fyght with his enmyes w^t whom alſo wẽt this northẽ man which ſhortly was ſmytẽ in ye hele w^t an arow wherfore he incõtynẽtly fell downe almoſt dede wherfore one of his felaws ſayd art thou he y^t art all hart and for ſo lytyll a ſtroke in the hele now art almoſt dede. To whom he anſweryd & ſayd by goddes ſale I is hard hed/ leggys/ body helys & all/ therfore ought not one to fere when he is ſtryken in ye hart.

c. *Of the burnyng of old John.*

The ſame ſtory is related in Kirchhof, " Wendunmuth," Frankf. 1573, No. 348, fol. 333 *verſo*, " Von einem hülzern Johannes;" and in C. F. Gellert's " Fabeln," buch iii. " Die Wittwe," Leipzig, 1836, p. 165.

IN a certayn towne there was a wyfe
somwhat agyd that had beryed her
husband whose name was callyd John/[1]
whom she loued so tenderly in his lyfe that after
his deth she causyd an ymage of tymber to be
made in vsage and person as lyke to hym as coude
be/ whiche ymage all day longe lay vnder her bed
and euery nyght she causyd her mayde to wrap
it in a shete & lay it in her bed & callyd it olde
John. This wyfe also had a prētyse whose name
was John/ whiche John wolde fayn haue weddyd
his mayſtres not for no grete pleasur but onely
for her good bycause she was rych/ wherfor he
imaginyd how he might obtayn his purpose &
spake to ye mayde of ye hous & desyryd her to
lay hym in his mayſtres bed for one nyght in
stede of the pycture/ & promysed her a rewarde
for her laboure/ which mayd ouer nyght wrappyd
ye sayd yōg mā in a shete & layd hym in his
mayſtres bed as she was wōt to lay ye pycture.

This wydow was wont euery nyght before she
slept & dyuers tymes whē she wakyd to kys the
sayd pycture of old John/ wherfore ye sayd nyght
she kyssyd ye sayd yong mā beleuyng that she had
kyst ye pycture/ & he sodēly start & toke her in
his armys and so well plesed her then/ that olde

[1] *was callyd John*] Hazl. was John.

Johñ from thēs forth was clene out of her mynde & was cõtent y^t this yonge Johñ ſholde lye w^t her ſtyll all y^t nyght & ye pycture of olde John ſholde lye ſtyl vnder ye bed for a thyng of nought. After this in ye mornynge this wydow intendyng to pleſe this yõg Johñ which had made her ſo good paſtyme all the nyght bad her mayd go dreſſe ſome good mete for theyr brekefaſt to feſt therwith her yõg Johñ/ this mayd whā ſhe had lõge ſought for wood to dres y^e ſayd mete told her maſtres y^t ſhe coud fynd no wood y^t was dry except onely ye picture of old Johñ y^t lyeth vnder ye bed/ thē quod ye wyf agayn/ fath[1] hym down & lay hym on ye fyre for I ſe well he wyll neuer do me good nor he wyll neuer do better ſeruyce though I kepe hym neuer ſo longe. So the mayd by her cõmaundemēt dreſſid ye brekfaſt/ & ſo olde Johñ was caſt out for nought & brent & from thens forth yong Johñ occupyed his place.

¶ By this tale ye may ſe it is no wyſdome for a mā to kepe longe or to chyryſhe that thyng y^t is able to do no pleaſure nor ſeruyce.[2]

[1] *fath*] i.e. fetch.
[2] The moral is wanting in Hazl.

¶ Finis.

¶ Thus endeth the booke of a .C. mery
talys. Empryntyd at London at the fygne of
the Merymayd At Powlys gate next
to chepe fyde. ¶ The yere
of our Lorde .M. v. C.
.xxvi. ¶ The .xxii.
day of Nouēber.

JOHANNES RASTELL.

¶ Cum preuilegio
Regali.

CHISWICK PRESS:—PRINTED BY WHITTINGHAM AND WILKINS,
TOOKS COURT, CHANCERY LANE.